Legendary
Yankee Stadium

Memories & Memorabilia From *the House that Ruth Built*

T.S. O'Connell
Editor of *Sports Collectors Digest*

Published by

krause publications
A subsidiary of F+W Media, Inc.

700 East State Street • Iola, WI 54990-0001
715-445-2214 • 888-457-2873
www.krausebooks.com

Our toll-free number to place an order or obtain
a free catalog is (800) 258-0929.

Cover artwork "Yankee Stadium,"
charcoal and pastel on paper by Andy Jurinko

Library of Congress Control Number: 2008937687

ISBN-13: 978-0-89689-935-3
ISBN-10: 0-89689-935-7

Cover Design by Paul Birling
Interior Design by Heidi Bittner-Zastrow
Edited by Justin Moen

Printed in China

Legendary *Yankee Stadium*

Contents

Act I
1923-46

Act II
1947-75

Act III
1976-2008

Photo by Ezra Shaw/Getty Images

Photo by John Iacono/Sports Illustrated/Getty Images

Yankee Stadium artwork by Andy Jurinko.

Foreword
by Marty Appel

Don't turn the page! My first impression as a kid entering Yankee Stadium in the 1950s was NOT the massive spread of green grass, so strange to an urban child.

Once I thought that was an original idea. Now, it seems everyone says it. I've read it so often, it almost makes the experience seem ordinary! So I've stopped saying it. (Although it was awfully impressive).

No, my first amazement and wonderment moment was science, something I knew little about at age seven, and about the same today. It was the whole "speed of sound" thing. I sat with my dad in the right field grandstand and marveled at how long the sound of the ball hitting the bat took to travel to our seats. I had vaguely heard of the speed of light and the speed of sound, but this was like attending the game with Don Herbert, "Mr. Wizard," of TV fame, for those old enough to remember.

Now I know that this phenomenon could have been replicated at any ballpark, maybe even little Baker Bowl in Philadelphia, but it was at Yankee Stadium that I first experienced it, and I never got over it. (When just a dozen years later I went to work for the team, I was privileged to watch the games from the press box, where all sounds were true to the moment and no delays were noticeable.

We couldn't hear the sound of the Lexington Avenue subway passing by on River Avenue even if we tried).

I continued to sit in the grandstand as I grew older, even when I was old enough to go on my own. For someone who would one day be writing all those promos about "plenty of good seats still available!" I was kind of an idiot when it came to buying tickets. Reserved seats were $2.50. And grandstand, the last rows, were $1.50. I thought you could only buy reserve seats in advance, ("reserving" them) by adding 25 cents to the total order for postage and handling, and making the purchase weeks ahead by mail. Even though the red ticket kiosks said reserved seats were $2.50, I assumed you could only buy grandstand on the day of the game, so that was where I put down my six quarters for a seat.

Now came the day I was actually interviewed for a job, to answer Mickey Mantle's fan mail. This was in 1967. The outside of the stadium had been painted white a year or so earlier (instead of the natural concrete color), the seats were dark blue (instead of the original light green), and the offices were in the ballpark (instead of at Fifth Avenue and 57th Street).

I entered through the familiar player's entrance, approximately even with where first base was situated, and then was escorted

The player entrance to the field at Yankee Stadium, sacred ground for any true Yankee fan.   Marty Appel photo

downstairs to the basement office of Bob Fishel, the team's PR director. Bob was a legend because he had been there since 1954, was the editor of the *Yearbook*, and frequently had his name mentioned by Mel Allen on TV. I knew what he looked like and I thought I was meeting a genuine celebrity. What a nice man he was, and he made me feel comfortable at once.

I couldn't help but look around his office. A Babe Ruth signed baseball, in a ball holder. A box of a dozen team-signed balls on the credenza next to his Royal typewriter. A framed front page of the *Cleveland Plain-Dealer* from the day he was born, May 15, 1914. Lots of sharpened No. 2 pencils, and boxes and boxes of unanswered fan mail. That was going to fall into my lap if the interview went well.

But I wasn't going to take any chances. Maybe I wouldn't get the job. I didn't know for sure as I left that day. So as I left the PR office to turn right up the stairs, something came over me compelling me to turn left, open the door right there, and perhaps "accidentally" peer into the Yankee clubhouse. What a moment that would be!

This Babe Ruth and Lou Gehrig signed ball sold for $98,600 in the May 2008 Robert Edward Spring Auction.

No good. It wasn't the clubhouse. That would be another 20 feet straight, 60 feet right, and 30 feet left, as I would later learn. Instead was a harsh sign on the concrete wall saying "ABSOLUTELY NO WOMEN BEYOND THIS POINT." Bold block letters, all caps. Nothing inviting about it.

I took it to mean that they were very serious on that subject, and that somehow it extended to anyone who didn't belong there, and I better not push my luck and wander any farther. I reversed course and headed back up the steps, past a painting of Wee Willie Keeler hitting one where it ain't.

Well, I did get hired, and I did answer Mickey's fan mail, and two years later became Fishel's full-time assistant, and five years later, the team's PR director, the youngest in major league history. Did it help that in the late 1960s I was one of the few my age who knew who Red Ruffing was traded for without looking it up? Probably. Most kids my age were not following baseball very closely at that time. (Cedric Durst!).

Working the fan mail shift (I like the way that sounds, like Joe Friday working the robbery division on "Dragnet"), I did of course partake in the routines of my fellow front-office colleagues at old Yankee Stadium, picking up lunch across the street at the Yankee Tavern, and on nice days when the team was on the road or playing at night, sitting in the empty stands, watching the grounds crew maintain the field, and listening to everyone play general manager by talking about the dead weight we needed to get rid of and the players we ought to trade for. The guys on the ground crew would take a break now and then to pass out football betting slips, if we were in season. (All Yankee employees got two tickets for Giants football games in those days, when the Giants played their games in "our place.")

The front office was perhaps 40 people, including the secretaries, switchboard operators and ticket staff. It really was its own small family and we all knew everything about each other. No one in an executive capacity had a marketing degree or carried a title having anything to do with broadcasting, publishing, promotion or community affairs. Our press guide, very modest by today's standards, was intentionally withheld from public sale so that the "media" – we still called them "the press," would have some information exclusive to them and not known by the fan at home. Such as how each batter hit, first half and second half, of the previous season.

The *Yankee Yearbook*, almost free of advertising, was intended to promote the team and Fishel always wanted it to cost less than a buck. You could always order it by mail at P.O. Box 1969, or whatever year it was. The post office loved us and cooperated in saving us that box number. The Yankee Stadium telephone number, Cypress 3-4300, was unchanged except for the area code, since it was assigned in 1952, and was still in force in 2008.

One of my first adventures on the field itself found me wandering into the outfield on a sunny lunch break, to stand where Mantle stood, to experience – my God! – where Babe Ruth stood.

I was surprised that the outfield was not perfectly level. It certainly seemed that way on television. Of course, it also seemed gray on television, not green. But it had little hills and valleys varying by a few inches here and there and was not as perfect as we now see watching football played on artificial turf. That was a surprise to me.

Looking up at the triple-deck seats was awesome. How in the world could an outfielder pick up a ball against that backdrop, especially

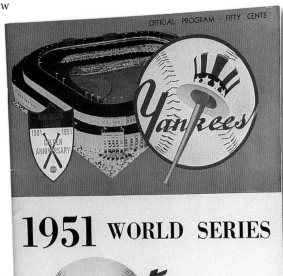

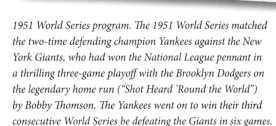

1951 World Series program. The 1951 World Series matched the two-time defending champion Yankees against the New York Giants, who had won the National League pennant in a thrilling three-game playoff with the Brooklyn Dodgers on the legendary home run ("Shot Heard 'Round the World") by Bobby Thomson. The Yankees went on to win their third consecutive World Series be defeating the Giants in six games.

crowded with fans in different colored clothing? And the enormity of the field was big enough for a dozen homes to be constructed – how could three guys cover all this?

Suddenly, I wanted to stand where Ruth stood, and for a moment, I didn't remember whether he played left or right! How could I not know such a thing?

It turns out, he played both of them, although chiefly right when he was at home. It had something to do with where the more difficult sun field was – and he played where it was less threatening. And right field in Yankee Stadium offered a smaller patch of real estate to cover. So at Yankee Stadium, he mostly played right. And I walked over there and stood where he had stood.

This was not really a feat that the common man couldn't experience. Being able to stand there alone in the empty park was the trick. Until the early 1960s, the fans would be allowed across the outfield and through the bullpens onto River Avenue as a way of exiting. They could walk over to the three monuments in dead center and check them out in all of their tarnished glory. They weren't allowed on the infield – the ushers stood protection, but they left "in an orderly fashion" with no efforts to tear up the sod for a souvenir. It was a different time.

I went hunting for the famous drain that Mantle had stumbled upon in the 1951 World Series, the one where his spikes caught, his knee buckled and DiMaggio called him off at the last second. Could such a drain be found in this enormous real estate? If so, it was beyond my ability. And I later learned that the drains had

been replaced with a safer drainage system.

I remember how smooth the infield dirt was, but that on occasion an infielder would reach down to remove a pebble. How, I wondered, could a pebble appear after nearly 50 years of playing there? Did they grow? How did they magically rise to the surface? How could a pebble escape five decades of manicuring? It remains a mystery to me, but then again, science wasn't my strong suit.

Yankee Stadium, as a functional office building apart from being a playing field, was essentially three usable levels – the basement, with our PR office, the two clubhouses, the press room, offices for electricians, plumbers, painters and grounds crew, and storage areas (where great treasures were discovered upon modernization after 1973), the street level, where the original Yankee clubhouse was built, and where the ticket office, accounting offices, and concessionaire offices stood, and the top level, where the president, GM and farm directors resided. The Stadium Club restaurant, which featured the framed retired uniform Nos. 3, (Ruth) 4, (Gehrig), and 5 (DiMaggio) in the lobby, was down the third base line on street level.

The concession stands didn't show much imagination. In those days, you could buy a yearbook, a scorecard, a pencil, a badge with Yogi or Mickey on it, a pennant, a baseball with facsimile auto-graphs, a 12-player picture pack (black-and-white), and maybe a cap. The Yanks were funny about caps. When someone went to general manager George Weiss one day and suggested "Cap Day," Weiss was said to have pounded his fist on his desk and said, "Do you think I want every kid in this city walking around with a Yankee cap?!"

Either Weiss was far from a marketing genius, or he foresaw the day when nearly everyone doing a perp walk on the local news had a Yankee cap on.

For the renovation, Fishel had suggested building non-baseball offices to lease to outside businesses who would pay plenty to have a Yankee Stadium address. It was an interesting idea that never came to be, just as the original idea of enclosing the entire field with three decks (the 1923 artist renderings showed that) never came to be.

Whatever other dreams were in the mind of Jacob Ruppert probably did come to be. If he dreamed that the team would win more world championships than anyone else in the 20th century, despite giving the rest of the teams a two-decade head start, he would have been right. The Yankees went pennant-less from their birth in 1903 as the Highlanders until 1921. He was also classy to name the place Yankee Stadium, instead of Ruppert Stadium.

I worked in Yankee Stadium until 1977, including the two years the team played at Shea Stadium during the renovation. When we returned in '76, my office looked like the George Costanza office on "Seinfeld," with windows overlooking the field. It may not have been the same ballpark structurally that the immortals played in, but it was the same patch of earth on which they stood. And there was not a day when I did not peer down and think about working in the same "office" as Ruth, Gehrig, DiMaggio and Mantle.

Credit Michael Burke, the team president during the CBS ownership years, with insisting that the façade design, which circled the old park, be retained as the décor over the billboards at the rear of the bleachers. In the early '70s, that design was not yet thought of as a "logo," nor held in reverence. He knew it when he saw it. In the end, it was a great contribution to the franchise's lore.

And yes, absolutely, credit George Steinbrenner with taking a storied franchise and making it even more legendary, acknowledging all that came before him, honoring the past while giving current day fans a fantastic on-field presentation worthy of exceeding Broadway prices. More stars, and a different ending each day.

My only beef with the reverence for the past is that pennant-winning seasons, as opposed to world championship-winning seasons, are treated as though the team finished last. All displays featuring the years of championships feature only the ones in which the World Series was won. I think it shortchanges the memories of great pennant-winning seasons. But who am I to quibble with Mr. Steinbrenner's record of success and attention to detail.

As for nostalgia today about moving north a block and leaving the old grounds behind, I take comfort in knowing that, oh, 50 years from now, they will probably tear down the "new" place and build another Yankee Stadium right where this one is. I hope they save the spot. And I hope my grandchildren experience the same feeling of awe when they notice the "speed of sound" thing, although I suspect they will be smarter and richer than me, and be able to plunk down a few thousand bucks for a reserved seat, not one in the grandstand.

Marty Appel is the author of 17 books, including "Now Pitching for the Yankees," *a personal memoir, and* "Munson," *a new biography of Thurman Munson, with whom he did an autobiography 30 years ago. He is also a featured columnist for* Sports Collectors Digest.

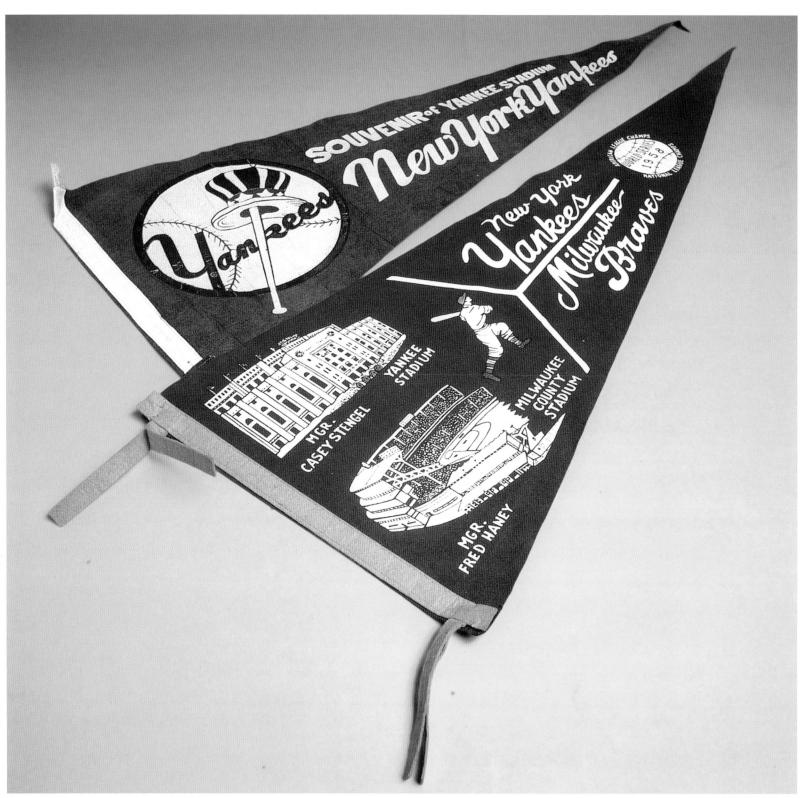

Souvenir pennants. (David Spindel Collection)

Introduction

And there used to be a ballpark
Where the field was warm and green
And the people played their crazy game
With a joy I'd never seen.
And the air was such a wonder
From the hot dogs and the beer
Yes, there used a ballpark, right here.

Written by Joe Raposo,
Nailed by Frank Sinatra

NEW YORK YANKEES · 1949 · WORLD CHAMPIONS

David Spindel Collection

The field at Yankee Stadium *was* warm and green, and for 84 seasons they played their crazy game there, and for much of that time they played with a joy like nobody had ever seen, a joy that came from winning more frequently, more impressively and more imperiously than any professional sports franchise has ever done before or since. This is the story of that ballpark, those men, their exploits, their heroics and occasional missteps, and even their anguish and disappointments.

There was less of those last two emotions than several generations of talented ballplayers would have any right to expect, but there was real anguish nonetheless. Despite performing feats of mythic proportion on the greatest sports stage in the greatest city in the world, and despite being regarded as much as figures from the Iliad as from the Baseball Register, these were real men, with all of the humanity – good and bad – that might be expected from any sampling of their times. But these men were Yankees ... and they played at Yankee Stadium!

For diehard American League fans from places like Kansas City, Washington, D.C., Cleveland, Boston, Detroit, Philadelphia and all the way to St. Louis, the hated Yankees from Yankee Stadium provided a good deal of *their* anguish and disappointment. The comparisons became cliche: the Yankees were Wall Street to the rest of the American League's Main Street. They were caviar in a profession built around the decidedly pedestrian hot dog. With a dynasty that took hold in the Roaring Twenties and flowered once again through much of the Great Depression, the Yankees were the

Ticket stubs from Roger Maris' 61st home run game in 1961 and from Don Larsen's perfect game in the 1956 World Series are shown (David Spindel Collection), along with a 1959 Topps Mickey Mantle card.

Rick Clarkson/Allsport

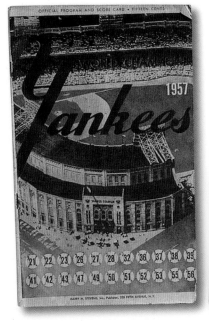
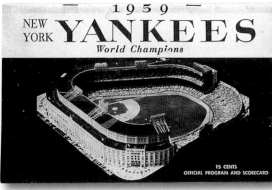
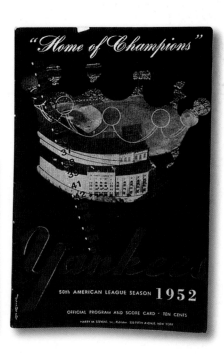

Yankees souvenir programs from 1957, 1959 and 1952.

yin and yang of an America that seemingly had lost its way.

The ball club represented great power and wealth, along with a dynamic preoccupation with that most American of desires: winning. At the same time, it managed all this initially behind the talents of a character who couldn't have been conjured up by Damon Runyon at his most imaginative. The Yankees were cold, efficient, regal and relentless; their star player was coarse, effusive, exuberant and uncontrollable. Ruth was revered by millionaires who weathered the hard-scrabble times with ease, just as he was applauded by the millions of the great unwashed who shuddered through a decade of deprivation, awaiting – as it turned out – a world war to come along and revive the economy and their fortunes.

So we will tell the stories of those great heroes, their games, their mischief and even occasional mayhem, and we'll do it all with a flourish that comes from a different direction. Like the archeologist who patiently pokes about in the ravine to find those pieces that answer his questions, we'll shed light on the lore and legend of a great stadium and the men who patrolled it by showing you the artifacts from their times, from their games, sometimes ancient, often not so ancient. From graying flannels, proud Adirondack lumber and yellowed baseballs to souvenir programs, baseball cards of every description and even the very stadium seats, these artifacts will tell the tales of these men and this now-demolished ballpark just as their owns words will.

There used to be a ballpark right here, and now there's a pretty nice one nearby. Time for some final stories from "The House That Ruth Built."

– T.S. O'Connell

"Yankee Stadium Panorama" by Andy Jurinko.   www.goodsportsart.com

Chapter 1

Yankee Stadium

Once upon a time the New York Yankees shared a cavernous stadium with their crosstown rivals the New York Giants. It wasn't really a baseball stadium at all: the Polo Grounds had originally been built for just that purpose, and thus its configuration for baseball, which began there in 1880, was odd indeed.

For much of the 10 seasons from 1913-22, it was your typical landlord/renter relationship, with the Giants pretty much looking down their collective noses at the Yankees. Led by John McGraw, their combative manager whose very managerial style dictated strategic and tactical thinking in Major League Baseball, the Giants were the first great dynasty in the game, winning 10 pennants in the first 25 years of the 20th century.

No such luck for their tenants, the Yankees, who languished in the middle of the American League standings for most of the decade, that is until a certain young pitcher/outfielder arrived from Boston.

The purchase of Babe Ruth changed just about everything, much of it in immediate fashion. With McGraw fuming off stage, the presence of Ruth in

1914 Baltimore News Babe Ruth rookie card.

1920 more than doubled Yankees attendance, going from 619,000 to 1,290,000.

And it was the way that Ruth and the Yankees did it that frosted McGraw's grommet: with the home run. The Giants' skipper had dominated the baseball landscape with a combination of uncanny pitching, timely hitting, hustling and generally relying on what was called "inside baseball" at the time and "small ball" 100 years later.

After socking an unheard of 29 home runs for the Red Sox in 1919, Ruth arrived in New York and found the curious dimensions of the Polo Grounds much to his liking. The 1920 season, played under the shadow of the infamous Black Sox Scandal World Series in 1919, saw Ruth up the single-season home run record to 54, and then again to 59 the following season.

Rather than grumbling about the demise of his brand of baseball, McGraw probably should have tried to steal the phenom from his tenants, but the

Yankees weren't about to make the same mistake the Red Sox did. With an unhappy and blustering landlord and a star player who clearly needed his own unfettered spotlight on the biggest stage in baseball, better they should build their own park.

The Yankees owner Col. Jacob Ruppert, who bought out co-owner Col. Tillinghast L'Hommedieu Huston in 1922, didn't think much of McGraw's suggestion that the club might emigrate to Queens, and ultimately settled on a 10-acre parcel just across the Harlem River in the South Bronx, the Astor estate, between 17th and 161st Streets, within sight of the Polo Grounds.

McGraw had suggested to Giants owner Charles Stoneham that the "Yankees will have to build a park in Queens or some other out-of-the-way place. Let them go away and wither on the vine."

That's not precisely what happened.

Built in less than a year at a cost of $2.5 million, the new ballpark opened on April 18, 1923, with the Yankees defeating the rival Red Sox in an historic game that included, appropriately enough, the inaugural home run by Ruth, a third-inning blast off Howard Ehmke.

The new stadium seated 58,000, but attendance, presumably inflated a bit, was reported at 74,217 for that game, with another 25,000 reportedly turned away.

Dubbed by *New York Evening Telegram* scribe Fred Lieb as "The House That Ruth Built," it would prove to have Bambino-friendly dimensions, most notably the 295 feet down the right field line that would be enticing for left-handed pull hitters for generations to come. Conventional wisdom holds that the cozy dimensions in right were incorporated to take advantage of the Babe's prowess; a more likely culprit would seem to be the simple architectural demands of the oddly shaped plot that they had to work with. Pushing back the right field wall would likely have reduced the capacity of the ball-park, something quite clearly not suited to the owner's wishes.

The park underwent some modest renovations in the late 1930s, replacing some wooden bleachers with concrete and shrinking Death Valley in left-center somewhat, though it would remain daunting enough to thoroughly aggravate the likes of the Great DiMaggio and

a number of other legendary right-handed power hitters.

By the 1950s, a number of changes took place that would pave the way for more renovations a decade later and ultimately the major refurbishment that would close the stadium down from 1974-75.

In 1953, as the club was wrapping up its fifth consecutive World Series title, owners Dan Topping and Del Webb sold the Stadium for $6.5 million to Earl and Arnold Johnson of Kansas City, Mo., the initial salvo in the development of an incestuous relationship between the Yankees and Johnson's Kansas City Athletics in the 1950s, when conventional baseball wisdom holds that a number of important trades were curiously one-sided in favor of the Bronx men.

By the late 1960s, the Stadium had already hoisted 27 American League pennants aloft (and 20 World Series flags, as well), but the grand old stadium was starting to deteriorate. And if the facility was going downhill, it was keeping pace with its environs, the South Bronx, which seemed to be declining in direct relation to the Yankees' position in the standings.

In 1964, the Yankees were sold to CBS and the Stadium underwent a $1.35 million facelift that included painting the building

1953 Bowman Color card of Billy Martin and Phil Rizzuto.

Courtesy Topps

white and much of the inside blue. Still, it was clear that more would have to be done.

With charismatic New York City Mayor John Lindsay in the middle of competing plans to perk up the grand old lady, debate heated up in 1971 over proposals that would increase Stadium seating, improve parking, remove obstructive girders and also provide funds for improvements to the surrounding area. In 1972, the Mayor announced that New York City would purchase Yankee Stadium for $24 million (numerically 10 times the original cost of construction, but closer to four times when adjusted for inflation), and then lease it back to the Yankees. The lease term was for 30 years, an arrangement necessary for the city's plan to develop "the most modern sports arena in the country."

Shea Stadium, home of the Mets, was also owned by the city, and after some wrangling with its principal tenant, a deal was worked out for the two clubs to share the friendly Flushing confines for the two years of the Yankee Stadium renovations.

Estimates started at around $28 million, but ultimately the Big Fix would run up a tab of $160 million. Removing the dreaded pillars that obstructed views (105 of them all told) actually reduced seating capacity to 57,500.

Despite that reduction, the idea was that the city-owned Stadium would generate more profit because the "new" facility would be more amenable to events other than just baseball. The accounting configuration would now include the city – en route to perhaps the greatest financial crisis it would ever face in the late 1970s – which would collect five percent of admissions, concessions and parking based on attendance of between 750,000 and 1.5 million and 10 percent above 1.5 million. And there would be a minimum payment of $200,000, a floor that would never become relevant.

The 10 percent would be in effect for the entire lease term and beyond: Yankee Stadium II attendance never descended below the 1.5 million threshold, not even in the icky, bastardized, strike-shortened year of 1981. Attendance totals of two million were essentially the norm virtually from the opening in 1976, and the three million

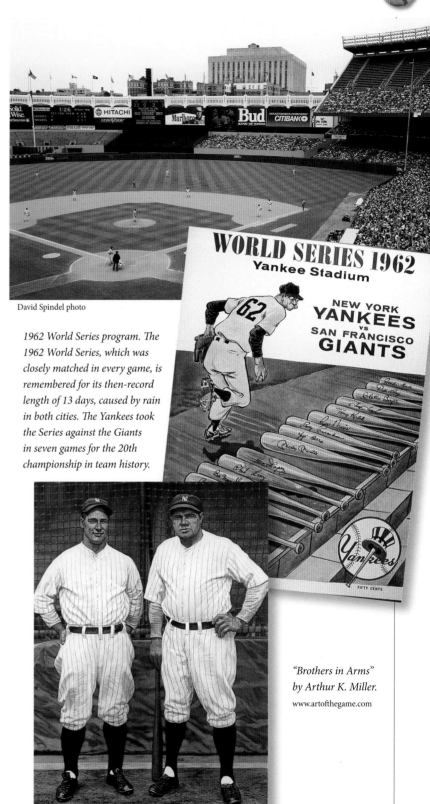

David Spindel photo

1962 World Series program. The 1962 World Series, which was closely matched in every game, is remembered for its then-record length of 13 days, caused by rain in both cities. The Yankees took the Series against the Giants in seven games for the 20th championship in team history.

"Brothers in Arms" by Arthur K. Miller.
www.artofthegame.com

barrier was cracked in 1999. The ball club topped the four million point in the final four years of the old park.

For Yankees fans, dismayed by an unprecedented streak of lackluster play on the field and the increasingly daunting challenge of confronting the, uh, urban decay of the area surrounding the Stadium, the renovation provided the following once a fan passed through the turnstile:

"In place of 64,644 wooden seats, the Stadium will hold 52,671 molded plastic ones in the dusky shade known as Yankee Blue," reported the *New York Times* in an Aug. 29, 1974 article. The bleachers would shrink from 11,000 to 2,500, and, in the *Times* words, "the arching frieze of sea-green copper that draped the top of the old stadium will echo faintly in pre-cast concrete trim above the new scoreboard."

New York Yankees button. (David Spindel Collection)
www.spindelvisions.com

Of course, fans got more than just that simulated copper frieze across the new 580-foot computerized scoreboard. Other new amenities included modern sodium-vapor ring lighting circling the stands on a new roof, a three-story parking garage for 750 cars, shortening of the outfield fences, the playing field was lowered by five feet, and there were escalators, private lounges (precursors to the ubiquitous luxury box of the modern era), and even the 120-foot Louisville Slugger outside Gate 4 – actually a boiler stack fitted to look like a bat, complete with a knob at the top, tape at the handle and Babe Ruth's facsimile signature on the barrel.

"The Bat" quite understandably became the ultimate meeting place for fans visiting the Stadium and was occasionally portrayed in exteriors of various "Seinfeld" episodes when the classic sitcom nearly "jumped the shark" by sending George

Costanza up to the Bronx to work for that other George. By the time the show's writers got around to poking fun at "The Boss," he had already done a pretty good job in the self-parody department.

The monuments, arguably the most famous historical treasures, were relocated with the renovation, moved beyond the outfield wall after a celebrated 25 years when the ghosts of Huggins, Ruth and Gehrig could quite literally find themselves working their magic once again as a ball in play pinballed from one to another while the base runner roared around the base paths.

The monuments' odd positioning didn't always help only the home team, or even the fastest runners. The author was on hand at the Stadium in 1968 to see Mantle bash his final triple, a scorching line drive that never seemed to get much more than 8-10 feet off the ground and was quickly rattling around between the stone monuments as the aging Mantle hobbled around the bases. I swear, it seemed like he was exasperated when he got to second and realized the quirky placement of the tributes was going to require him to push on to third.

1936 World Champions. (David Spindel Collection)

For the record, the retired numbers are:

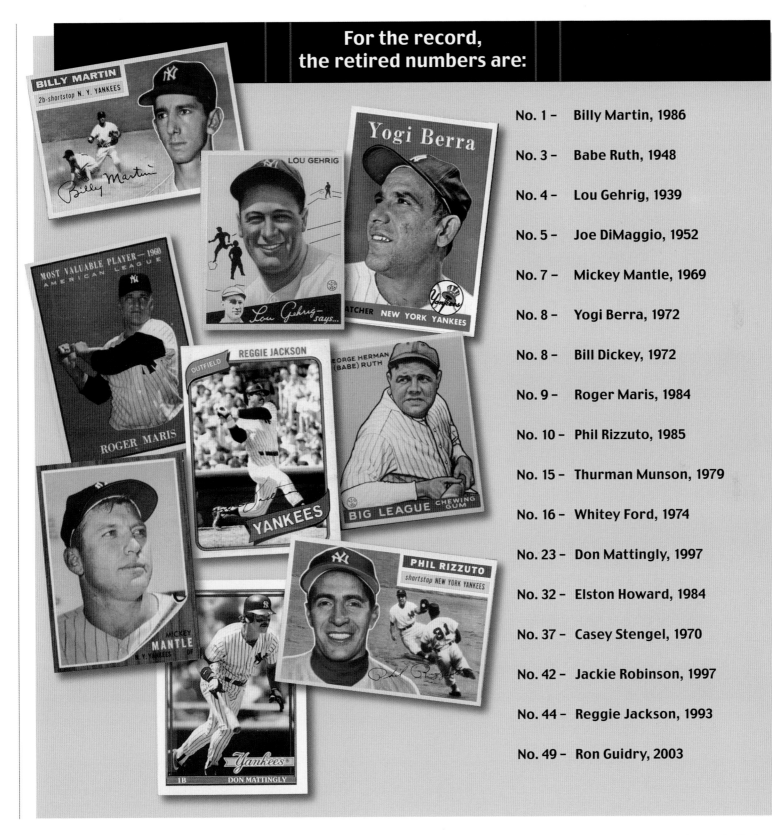

No. 1 – Billy Martin, 1986

No. 3 – Babe Ruth, 1948

No. 4 – Lou Gehrig, 1939

No. 5 – Joe DiMaggio, 1952

No. 7 – Mickey Mantle, 1969

No. 8 – Yogi Berra, 1972

No. 8 – Bill Dickey, 1972

No. 9 – Roger Maris, 1984

No. 10 – Phil Rizzuto, 1985

No. 15 – Thurman Munson, 1979

No. 16 – Whitey Ford, 1974

No. 23 – Don Mattingly, 1997

No. 32 – Elston Howard, 1984

No. 37 – Casey Stengel, 1970

No. 42 – Jackie Robinson, 1997

No. 44 – Reggie Jackson, 1993

No. 49 – Ron Guidry, 2003

And the plaques go to
(chronologically, from Ruppert in 1940 to Ruffing in 2004):

Jacob Ruppert, Ed Barrow, Joe McCarthy, Casey Stengel, Thurman Munson, Roger Maris, Elston Howard, Phil Rizzuto, Billy Martin, Whitey Ford, Lefty Gomez, Bill Dickey, Yogi Berra, Allie Reynolds, Don Mattingly, broadcaster Mel Allen, public address announcer Bob Sheppard, Reggie Jackson, Ron Guidry, and Red Ruffing.

In addition, there are plaques of Pope Paul VI in 1965 and Pope John Paul II in 1979. The final plaque denotes the famed Yankees "NY" insignia, which adorns the floor of the park's entrance.

The ceremonial plaques at the Stadium's Monument Park. Players consider receipt of a ceremonial plaque in Monument Park to be a supreme distinction. The ceremonial monuments themselves are the highest honor of all, and are awarded posthumously.

Photo by Ezra Shaw/Getty Images

With the renovation, Monument Park was built, eventually to have another stone added of Mickey himself, followed by DiMaggio and, on the first anniversary in 2002, a commemoration of the events of Sept. 11, 2001. The whole Monument Park will be recreated in the new stadium, all six stone monuments, 23 plaques and 16 retired numbers (for 17 players: No. 8 was retired twice, for Berra and Bill Dickey). Jackie Robinson is the only non-Yankee to have his number retired; this was done by all teams at the direction of Major League Baseball in 1997 on the occasion of the 50th anniversary of Robinson's breaking the color line in 1947.

At the time the "artifacts" from the old Yankee Stadium were dispersed hither and yon, the baseball memorabilia hobby/industry was in its infancy, so the prices represented bargains in the extreme.

An advertisement in the *New York Daily News* in May of 1974 offered one of those wood-slat Yankee Stadium seats for $7.50, "plus five empty Winston crush-proof boxes." Collectors with enough moxie to have snagged a straight-backed or curved-back seat at such a bargain price could simply pick up their treasure at their local E.J. Korvettes department store. The author smoked enough Winstons in the 1970s, cough, to have glommed his own section at Yankee Stadium, but alas, doesn't recall seeing that particular advertisement, even though he was living in New York at the time.

Thus, I did not wind up with a Stadium artifact that might sell for thousands of dollars today by ponying up a mere $7.50 in 1974. According to author Michael Gershman in his acclaimed book "*Diamonds: The Evolution of the Ballpark*," many others – including former Yankees and Hall of Famers – would display the foresight that I lacked.

Stan Musial reportedly snagged a bleacher seat in that 1974 sale that included bricks for $10 each, turnstiles for $100, a Gate A sign

Original Yankee Stadium seat.

at $300 and a hot dog vendor's tray for $5. Whitey Ford, Yogi Berra and Jim Bouton all bought box seats, and Bouton even tossed in a clubhouse stool and a large photo of Babe Ruth. Five-time Yankee manager Billy Martin ended up the proud owner of two stairs and a bannister from the dugout, though baseball historians might postulate that he more appropriately might have wound up with a nice plastic bag filled with dirt from the environs of home plate.

As serious fans know, Ruth's locker (and Gehrig's and Joe DiMaggio's) went upstate to the Baseball Hall of Fame in Cooperstown, and the Smithsonian received the Yankees' bat rack and bullpen steps, some VIP chairs and a ticket kiosk. Home plate went to Babe Ruth's widow; first base to Mrs. Gehrig. One box seat even made its way to Gracie Mansion, the mayor's residence in New York City. The foul poles had reportedly found new fair territory (remember, they are actually "fair") across the Pacific in Osaka, Japan; the stadium lights were sold for $30,000 and reportedly then resold to various Little Leagues around the country.

Yankees pennant. (David Spindel Collection)

Sports Collectors Digest columnist Paul Ferrante theorized in a March 14, 1997 article that perhaps the most intriguing casualty of the renovation process was a massive stack of some 20,000 unanswered fan letters to Mickey Mantle. "Given the pre-collecting boom tenor of 1974, it's fun to imagine how many Mantle rookie cards (or better yet, his 1952 Topps card) may have been in the pile awaiting autographs. Fifty? A hundred maybe? Only the incinerator knows for sure," he mused.

An intriguing notion, for sure, but no less of an authority than Marty Appel, hired by the Yankees in 1967 for that very purpose of responding to the tsunami of Mick mail, can't remember any such pile remaining by 1974, by which time he had ascended to the role of PR director.

Gershman tallied up the total from the sale at around $300,000, which was a pretty good slice of what the Stadium originally cost to build. That would also buy you about two games worth of Alex Rodriguez's services, maybe 10 official at bats, or, to put it in more fan-friendly terms, 37,500 warm, flat, 16-ounce Ballantine beers at the ballpark.

New York Yankees commemorative bats.
(David Spindel Collection)

Yankees souvenir pennant. (David Spindel Collection)

1923 World Series ticket.
(David Spindel Collection)

Thurman Munson batting helmet.
(David Spindel Collection)

"Yankee Stadium Panorama" by Andy Jurinko (detail).

Chapter 2

Managing in Gotham

The age-old debate about the relative importance of the manager vs. that of the ballplayers themselves never gets a better test than it does in the Big Apple. From the diminutive Miller Huggins trying to tame the brightest star in the game at the opening of Yankee Stadium in 1923 to Joe Torre grimly undertaking a balancing act like no other manager in history in the closing seasons of the Stadium at the dawn of the 21st century, being the skipper of the Yankees is a challenge.

Blessed with the contributions of literally dozens of Hall of Famers over that 85-year span – and managing the league's marquee franchise under a pressure unlike anywhere else – the men who managed the Yankees were expected to win by both management and the fans. It had not always been that way, since the team foundered for much of its first two decades in the fledgling American League, but by the time a certain Mr. Ruth arrived in 1920, expectations had changed. Tiny Miller Huggins, newly arrived in the Bronx for the 1918 season after a successful career as a top-flight second baseman for the Cardinals and later as their manager, would begin the dynasty that would essentially last for 40 years.

Over the years the managers for the Yankees were as different and diverse as their lineups ... and then some. Huggins, nicknamed "Hug," or more commonly, "Mighty Mite," was the prototypical scrappy, combative ballplayer who parlayed those attributes into nearly unmatched success as the Yankees' manager.

The man who had seemingly lassoed Babe Ruth – or at least enough to allow the Great Ruth to be just that – died tragically in 1929 of blood poisoning after an infection became visible under his right eye. He was 50. The league canceled all games the next day as thousands of tearful fans shuffled past his coffin at Yankee Stadium.

The man who had taken the

1980-2001 Perez-Steele
Hall of Fame Postcard Series.

team to six World Series and won three of them had also been at the helm of what is still widely described as the greatest team of all time. Mere mention of the 1927 Yankees conjures up visions of Murderer's Row and the incredible seasons that Ruth and younger teammate Lou Gehrig put together as the Yankees won 110 games and swept the Pirates in the World Series, but it was Huggins who had put it all together and kept it intact despite the considerable distractions that always loomed.

Arriving in 1918, it was the merging of the baseball savvy of the "Mighty Mite" Huggins with the business acumen (and Steinbrenner-like deep pockets) of a pair of Colonels: Jacob Ruppert and Tillinghast L'Hommedieu Huston, that set into motion a baseball dynasty that would essentially endure for more than four decades.

Add to the mix Hall of Fame executive Ed Barrow, who had been the manager of the rival Red Sox, but followed Babe Ruth to the Yankees, albeit one year later, and the management pieces were in place. At the end of the 1919 season, Huggins urged his bosses to pursue the Bosox slugger, and the rest, as they say, is history.

But, of course, it wasn't just the Babe that Huggins would have at his disposal. The Yankees, still playing at the Polo Grounds with McGraw as their landlord in 1921 and 1922, would win American League pennants, the first two in team history, but that first World Series crown would await the opening of Yankee Stadium in 1923. The Yankee ball club that would finally defeat McGraw's Giants, four games to two, would look decidedly different from the one he inherited in 1918.

Slugging Bob Meusel arrived in 1921, Lou Gehrig and Earle Combs in 1925; and Tony Lazzeri one year later. Murderer's Row was in place, and the team would show it: three consecutive pennants from 1926-28, and World Series sweeps of the Pirates and the Cardinals in the last two years after narrowly losing in seven games to St. Louis in 1926.

And then, as the ball club stumbled in 1929 and yet another powerhouse in the Philadelphia Athletics emerged, Huggins died suddenly in the final weeks of the regular season. By that time the Athletics had already clinched the pennant; the juggernaut – led by a trio of Hall of Famers in the everyday lineup (Jimmie Foxx, Al Simmons and Mickey Cochrane, and the best pitcher on the planet, Lefty Grove) – would rule the American League until the Yankees returned to the top of the heap in 1932.

It wasn't that the Yankees were bad during that drought, merely that the A's were very, very good ... and better. And the Bronx crew was showing signs of age, most notably Ruth, now in his mid-30s, though still nearly as productive as ever. Meusel, however, was sold to Cincinnati following the 1929 season, and Lazzeri had fallen off a bit in 1931 as well, but it wasn't the Yankees offense that caused the demise. At a time when whole leagues were batting .300, the dominance of the A's came from that aforementioned pitching staff.

After a year with Bob Shawkey as Yankees manager in 1930 and a third-place finish in the standings, Col. Ruppert brought in Joe McCarthy in 1931 in a move that was dogged by controversy from the start. Ruppert's aging star, Ruth, fancied himself managerial material,

Yankees manager Miller Huggins found himself pitted against his former team in the 1926 and 1928 World Series. (Programs from the David Spindel Collection)

1980-2001 Perez-Steele Hall of Fame Postcards of Joe McCarthy and Casey Stengel are shown top and center; Stengel painting by Andy Jurinko (bottom).

a notion probably not universally shared in the front office or even beyond.

"Marse Joe," as he would come to be known, would pretty quickly bring the club back to the World Series in 1932. With the nation in the throes of the Great Depression and attendance at the Stadium (and elsewhere) cut nearly in half from an astonishing 1930 peak of almost 1.2 million, McCarthy would be faced with the challenges of Ruth at the end of the line and yet another emerging power in the American League: the Detroit Tigers.

The Yankees finished second behind the Tigers in 1934-35, but returned to the World Series in 1936 with the arrival of one Joseph Paul DiMaggio to New York City by way of San Francisco.

With yet another Hall of Famer now duly installed in the Yankees' outfield, McCarthy would be rewarded with seven more pennants and another six World Series crowns, which was more than enough to earn him a spot in the Hall of Fame (1957). A vote as the third-best manager of all time would come with that 1969 celebration of baseball's centennial; by the time he walked away from the Yankees in 1946 after a beef with new owner Larry MacPhail, McCarthy was the all-time leader in wins with 1,460 and winning percentage at .615.

The Yankees would stumble to a third-place finish in that first year after the close of World War II, but rebounded to yet another pennant in 1947 behind newly installed manager Bucky Harris. When the Red Sox and

Indians surged to the top of the AL heap in 1948, Yankees ownership, now sans MacPhail, who had been bought out by Dan Topping and Del Webb a year earlier, GM George Weiss made as bold a managerial move as the game had ever witnessed.

Casey Stengel's ascension to the manager's position for the Yankees in 1949 has to remain one of the most daring managerial appointments ever. When he took over the team he made the observation, without any of the Stengelese that would be his trademark: "There is less wrong with this team than any team I have ever managed." Given to the mangled, hilarious non sequitur more notably than he was to understatement, this rare bit of Stengel's serious side would prove prophetic.

Much to the dismay of much of the baseball establishment, Stengel would orchestrate perhaps the greatest streak of world championships in the history of professional sports.

He would win 10 pennants and seven World Series crowns in just 12 seasons before being unceremoniously unloaded himself, along with Weiss, after the devastating loss to the Pirates in the 1960 World Series.

Because of his eccentric nature and his penchant to lapse into his world-famous Stengelese, he would suffer as much as any Yankees manager from the notion that just about anybody could manage such an all-powerful aggregation of talent. Ironically, his tenure as skipper in the Big Apple was hardly a smooth one or certainly not one suited to being a "pushbutton manager," and he patched together winning combinations and platoons with a deft touch that belied the often buffoonish image portrayed in the press.

Ousted after that World Series loss at Forbes Field in 1960, the Yankees managerial reins were

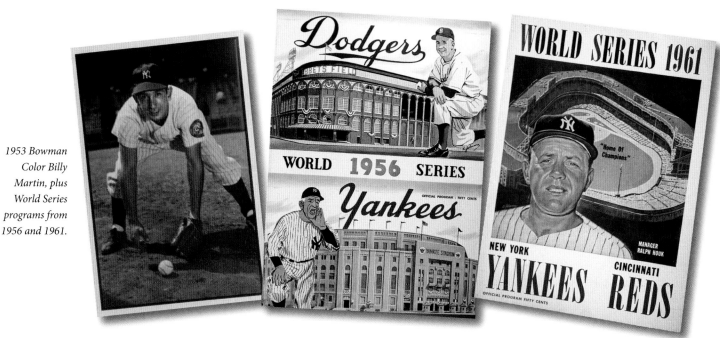

1953 Bowman Color Billy Martin, plus World Series programs from 1956 and 1961.

turned over to Ralph Houk, who found himself at the helm of a still potent but clearly aging juggernaut.

But those cracks certainly weren't visible in his first season at he helm as the Yankees dominated in the first expansion season in six decades of American League play. His ball club won 109 games and then promptly stomped the Cincinnati Reds in the World Series. To the untrained eye, it looked like the start of yet another dynasty, or more precisely, the continuation of the old one.

And indeed, the pennants kept on coming, in 1962 and 1963, but the 1962 World Series win would be the club's last for 15 years, though nobody could have imagined such a preposterous notion at the time. The hated Dodgers, once a handy metro rival, had moved to the West Coast in 1958, but had already won pennants in 1959 and 1963, sweeping the Yankees in four games that year in a drubbing that was a harbinger of things to come.

But in 1963 it was merely a source of agitation for Yankees brass, which booted Houk upstairs to the general manager position and planted its Hall-of-Fame catcher, Yogi Berra, in the dugout as manager for 1964. Like the hiring of Stengel 15 years earlier, it seemed an odd choice, almost as if Yankees hierarchy was atoning for passing on its first opportunity to hire a seemingly ill-suited star when it rebuffed the Babe's entreaties to manage at the end of his career.

Yogi fared well enough in that 1964 campaign, guiding a late-season 11-game winning streak that finally nudged the Yankees atop the standings in a heated pennant race. The National League's race had been even tighter, and the eventual champions, the St. Louis Cardinals, stopped the Bronx Bombers in a thrilling seven-game series that would begin the legend of one Bob Gibson at the same time that Mickey Mantle clubbed his last three World Series homers.

And just like that it was all done. Yogi had departed after the 1964 World Series; he had been replaced by the man who had guided the Cardinals: Johnny Keane. But the crusty Keane was climbing aboard a thoroughbred that had nothing left, and the Yankees would fall below .500 and into sixth place in 1965, then startle the baseball faithful yet again the following year with a 10th and last-place finish. This was unheard of and not be tolerated, and yet it would have to be tolerated nonetheless, awaiting only the arrival of a certain egomaniacal shipbuilding magnate in 1973. Even then, the change of ownership from CBS to George Steinbrenner would hardly be an instant success. It required a lot of tinkering, with players, managers and ultimately with the understanding of the new financial structure of the game of baseball itself.

Pushed out early in the 1966 season, Keane would hand the reins back to Houk, but that was hardly a solution to write home about.

The decorated World War II veteran would direct the team's fortunes, such as they were, until 1973. The next year Bill Virdon would be brought in, and the club showed signs of life, finishing second behind one of the American League's heirs apparent, the Baltimore Orioles.

The Yankees' resurgence would stall a bit in 1975, and Steinbrenner would reveal a genuine aversion to patiently waiting for the results he wanted. One of the Yankee heroes from the 1950s, Billy Martin, was brought in to push the team over that final hill. It was a tactical move that would get a bit overworked as the decade wore on, working just enough to be regarded as intermittent reinforcement, one of the most powerful and widely misunderstood forces in the universe.

As the silly soap opera of George and Billy unfolded in the mid-1970s, the first full year of Martin at the helm produced a drought-ending pennant. While the return to the Fall Classic was a welcome note to beleaguered Yankees fans who had endured the most difficult stretch in the team's history in the Bronx, the 1976 edition was rudely swept in four games by the final can of whoop-ass in the Big Red Machine. Steinbrenner, briefly thrilled by the glow of a pennant, was appalled by the four-game World Series debacle at the hands of Cincinnati. Something would have to be done.

The seeds of the solution had been sown a couple of years earlier, when a bit of contractual bungling had freed Catfish Hunter from the constraints of Charlie Finley and the Oakland A's.

Baseball fans got a preview of what was to come in the post-reserve-clause age with the almost unseemly circus of Hunter's signing at Christmas time in 1975. After arbitrator Peter Seitz ruled on Dec. 13, 1974, that Finley's failure to pay $50,000 of deferred compensation had voided Hunter's contract and thus made him a free agent, 11 days of bidding for Catfish's services ensued in an orgiastic frenzy the likes of which had never been imagined.

Just after Christmas, Steinbrenner's reported $3.75 million offer ($1 million signing bonus) prevailed, and a generation's worth of ballplayers got a glimpse of the kind of dollars the top rung could command. If it wasn't a brave new world, it was at least a very pricey one.

So the Yankees owner wasted no time following the 1976 World

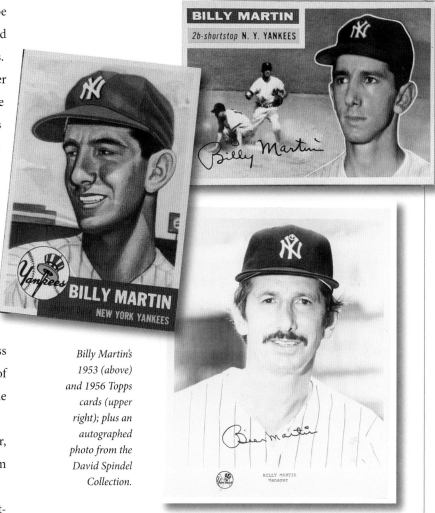

Billy Martin's 1953 (above) and 1956 Topps cards (upper right); plus an autographed photo from the David Spindel Collection.

Series drubbing in signing Reggie Jackson, the guy the gods had in mind when they devised the idea of a "free agent," to a near $3-million contract over five years. It left most of the baseball world speechless.

Ironically, it left the man likely to benefit the most from the addition of Jackson to the Yankees lineup less than thrilled, even if he had to toe the company line in at least feigning official enthusiasm. Billy Martin would clash with his new superstar almost from the start, highlighted by a mid-season tangle in the Yankees dugout between the two that was nicely captured by a national television feed in the pre-cable days of the 1970s.

We'll save much of the Billy-Reggie soap opera stuff for Reggie's own chapter, but suffice it say that the almost Shakespearean saga (alternately tragic and comic) between the volatile triumvirate would sustain Yankee fans for several years and contribute mightily to Martin's five firings and resulting dramatic reinstatements at the helm.

If Yankee fans could occasionally get confused whether Billy was coming or going, the club managed to persevere and win the World Series in 1977-78, and later a really icky mini pennant in 1981 as a result of the ghastly machinations done by MLB following the mid-season labor stoppage.

And for those who feel there's something to be said for managerial stability (think Walt Alston with the Dodgers from 1958-76), here's the quick breakdown of Yankee managers from Billy's first firing midway through 1978 to the arrival of Joe Torre in 1996: Dick Howser, Bob Lemon, Martin, Howser, Gene Michael, Lemon, Michael, Clyde King, Martin, Yogi Berra, Martin, Lou Piniella, Martin, Piniella, Dallas Green, Bucky Dent, Stump Merrill and Buck Showalter. Whew!

I suspect it's up to individual fans whether that recitation constitutes tragedy or comedy, but either way, it didn't translate to a lot of success on the field. Howser would snag a divisional title in 1980 when the Yankees won 103 games but got swept by the Royals in the playoffs, and Showalter would guide the Yankees to the best record in the American League in 1994 when MLB shot itself in the foot (and a Wild Card berth the following year), but that's all the hardware the club has to show for that curious merry-go-round of mangers. Stability, in the name of Joe Torre, would change all of that.

After a standout 18-year playing career in the National League, Torre moved from first base at Shea Stadium into the manager's role after Joe Frazier (the non-smoking Frazier) was fired early in the 1977 campaign.

In 14 years as a manager in the National League for the same teams that employed him as a player, Torre was well regarded if less than spectacular, winning a division title with Atlanta in 1982 for his sole post-season effort.

It may have been little more than bad timing: Torre left the Mets

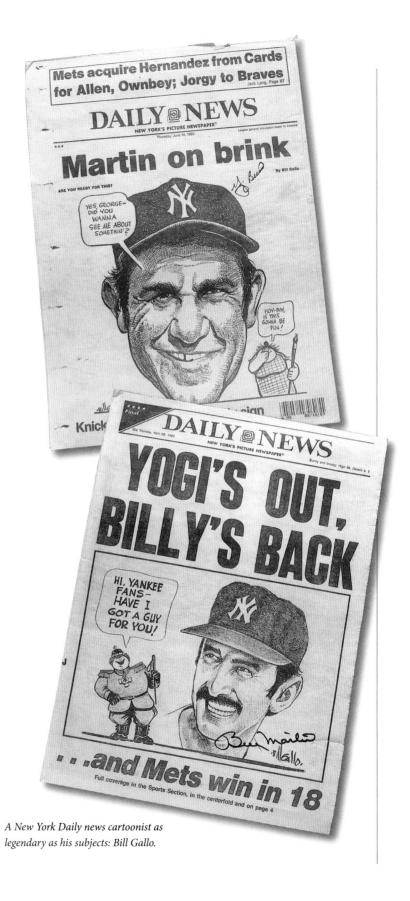

A New York Daily news cartoonist as legendary as his subjects: Bill Gallo.

Joe Torre. During his tenure as manager from 1996-2007, the Yankees reached the playoffs each year, won 10 American League East Division titles, six American League pennants, and four World Series titles, in addition to compiling a .605 winning percentage.

a couple of years before Darryl Strawberry and Dwight Gooden would help bring the club to prominence in the mid-1980s, and took over the reins at St. Louis just as the stellar 1980s Cardinals powerhouse was breaking up.

But Joe's timing in 1996 was as good as it gets. On a team curiously devoid of the kind of marquee names that had been the hallmark of earlier Yankees dynasties, here was a ball club that was solid up and down the order, with a pitching staff and everyday lineup nicely divided between young and old.

Center fielder Bernie Williams was in his prime at 27, as was first baseman Tino Martinez, but it was a youngster, 22-year-old Derek Jeter, who would quickly emerge as a team leader and, arguably, the rock upon which a great dynasty would be built. Though Jeter was a known talent in 1996, his first full campaign in the majors, no one could have predicted the dominance to come from the Bronx Bombers as the millennium came to a close.

Torre, often rudely treated by the New York press corps in the beginning, would win four World Series crowns in his first four years. The only miss during that span was 1997, when a Wild Card berth earned them a divisional series thumping by Cleveland, 3 games to 2.

The giddy five-year stretch peaked in the middle: the 1998 club racked up a record 114 wins, then whizzed through the playoffs with an 11-2 record, including a four-game World Series sweep of the Padres. The next year the wins settled in at a less other-worldly 98, but the postseason was a breeze yet again, 11-1, with another World Series sweep, this time against the Braves.

In 2000, in a much-ballyhooed Subway Series against the cross-town rival Mets, the Yankees would win again, 4 games to one.

From 2001-07, at the end of Torre's tenure, the Yankees would wind up in postseason play all seven years, even losing the World Series twice, in 2001 and 2003. It marked a run of 13 straight years making the playoffs and 10 divisional titles. But the success of the last half of the 1990s decade put the bar perhaps impossibly high.

Despite winning more than 100 games each season from 2002-04, there was only one World Series trip in that span, and that a losing effort to the Florida Marlins, 4 games to 2.

And the postseason offered further indignities for Yankees fans: in 2004, the hated Red Sox would come back from an 0-3 deficit to take the ALCS from the Yankees in seven games, and then go on to win the World Series, ending the "Curse of the Bambino" and giving the Bosox their first title in 86 years. After the Yankees surrendered their streak of nine AL East crowns in 2007, dumped by the Sox again, the man who used to fire managers faster than kiss a duck stepped up his already full-fledged campaign of raising doubts about his now-beloved skipper.

So while the Red Sox were drubbing the Colorado Rockies in four games, George and Joe were competing for tabloid headlines as the wrangling over whether the Yankees' one-year, $5-million contract (plus the potential for $1-million in performance clauses) was appropriate for a manager of Torre's now-exalted status.

By the time the Red Sox had wrapped up their victory parade in downtown Boston, Torre had signed his reported three-year, $13-million deal to work his magic on the West Coast for the Dodgers. George's most stable (and successful) relationship with a major league manager had ended on a rocky note.

With little fanfare, the Yankees signed Joe Girardi in late October to manage for 2008-11. The 2008 Yankees finished out of the money (read playoffs) for the first time in 13 years. The Steinbrenner reins have been largely passed to sons Hank and Hal, so it will be interesting to see if the managerial musical chairs might start up again. Could it get any goofier with two guys calling the tunes?

Stay tuned.

Chapter 3

Babe Ruth

The Sporting News

George (Babe) Ruth, Yankees, P-OF, 1924   4

1981 Sporting News Conlon Collection

Close your eyes and imagine Michael Jordan, Muhammad Ali and Tiger Woods all rolled into one. That's Babe Ruth. Eighty years ago, major league ballplayers used to say their prayers at night by thanking the Almighty for all that he had provided, and then they would thank Babe Ruth for his not inconsiderable contribution to their welfare as well.

Michael, Ali and Tiger should probably save a mumbled word or two for The Bambino before they float off to the blissful sleep of the multimillionaire. When that remarkable triumvirate molded themselves into the sporting and marketing dynamos that they have become, they at least had a prototype to work from: Ruth. A 1999 ESPN poll ranked Ruth the third-greatest U.S. athlete of the century, behind Jordan and Ali. Uh, huh.

By the time Ruth was sold to the New York Yankees for $125,000 in 1920, he had already established himself as one of the biggest stars in the game. The left-hander had pieced together an 89-46 lifetime log with a 2.28 ERA, and would have seemed to be headed to Cooperstown and the Hall of Fame had there been such a thing in 1920.

But the Yankees had other designs on the 24-year-old. Arguably the last genuine two-way player in the game, Ruth had led the American League in home runs in his final two Boston seasons, including an unheard-of record of 29 in 1919. New York City sportswriters positively swooned over his prospects in swinging at the short right field wall at the Polo Grounds in Manhattan. They didn't know the half of it.

The newest Yankee socked 54 homers in his debut season, leading the league for the third time ... with nine more such accolades to come. When it was over, following 15 seasons in the Bronx and an awkward, Favre-like final orphan season with the Boston Braves in 1935, Ruth had nailed down his designation as the greatest player in history. One year later, he was voted into the Baseball Hall of Fame, still on the drawing board in the tiny hamlet of Cooperstown, N.Y. It would open officially three years later, and just as he was during his playing career, Ruth would be the star, head and shoulders above all others.

Indeed, the legacy of Babe Ruth is so much more expansive and elaborate than a mere compilation of his unmatched batting skills or his bigger-than-life persona and reckless disregard for the conventions of mere mortals. He had almost single-handedly transformed Major League Baseball from a rough-and-tumble contest highlighting speed, timely hitting and pitching to one that relied upon and glorified the ball struck savagely and thoroughly ejected from the premises. The game would never look back, nor would the millions of fans who quickly fell in love with power baseball and its principal practitioner.

Portrayed in several hammy silent movies, some of which he appeared in as himself, the Ruthian legend grew to epic proportions from a delicious mixture of myth and mayhem, all seasoned by a band of sportswriters eager to portray him in Herculean fashion.

From a called shot that may never have really happened in the 1932 World Series (who cares what the truth is?) to the apocryphal stories of swatting home runs for star-struck young boys gasping for breath on their deathbed, a legend was created that was infinitely bigger than any that had come before it. There were songs written about him, with records and sheet music sold to an adoring public.

Because of his enormous popularity, Ruth wound up with his name being affixed to hundreds of products, many of which survive in some quantity to this day, a testament to his unrivaled status in the collecting world. Pins, buttons, dolls, statues of every material and description, calendars, games, baseball equipment and pennants. He even wound up with his own brand of underwear, which turns up with admirable frequency at the major sports memorabilia auctions around the country. Call it the hobby that Ruth built.

Mickey Mantle may be the King of Cards, but the modern sports memorabilia hobby almost certainly has anointed Ruth with that

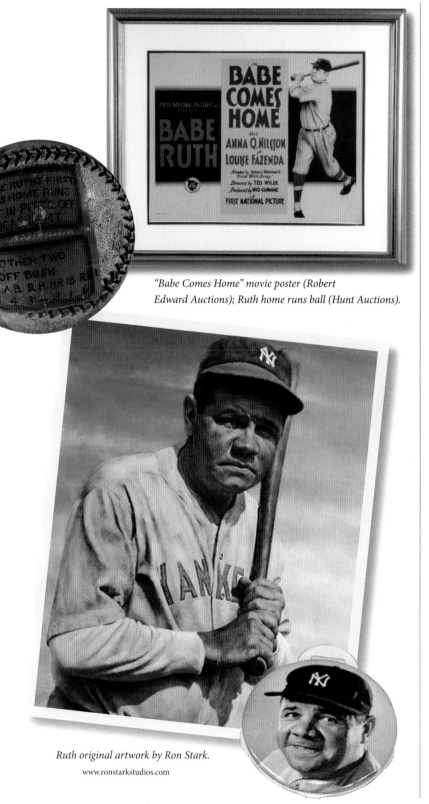

"Babe Comes Home" movie poster (Robert Edward Auctions); Ruth home runs ball (Hunt Auctions).

Ruth original artwork by Ron Stark.
www.ronstarkstudios.com

designation for photos, bats, balls, jerseys, and the like. And Ruth might have been the King of Cards too, except that for much of his heyday in the 1920s there simply weren't all that many baseball cards produced, at least not the kind that have captured widespread interest among casual hobbyists nearly a century later.

Still, his cards remain hobby treasures for advanced collectors, including an aesthetically humble "rookie card" that sold recently at auction for $517,000. Ruth's 1933 Goudey cards, coming near the end of his career yet headlining the most popular gum card set of the Depression era, are also iconic bits of cardboard, routinely selling for $100,000 and more in their highest grades.

The Ruthian lore had as much to do with his unique relationship to fans in general and children in particular. All loved him for his flamboyance and his gargantuan appetites as much as for his baseball skills, and he returned the affection. Lee Allen, a Ruth biographer, estimated that just by the time Ruth got to New York in 1920, he had already signed perhaps 5,000 or more photographs for children who had written to him.

But for serious fans and collectors, when the topic of Babe Ruth memorabilia comes up, the first thought may be the single-signed baseball. How could a mortal man sign so many baseballs and yet they are among the most expensive treasures available to serious hobbyists?

Single-signed Ruth balls are hardly rare; he would sign hundreds every year while he was playing, and many hundreds more in the years between his retirement in 1935 and his death from throat cancer on Aug. 16, 1948.

The orphan from St. Mary's Industrial School for Boys may not have been a great student, but he must have paid great

Ruth artwork by Arthur K. Miller; bust, alarm clock and board game from the David Spindel Collection.

Original Ruth Hartland Statue, personal check, pulp magazine and New York Daily Mirror from Aug. 17, 1948.

attention in his penmanship studies. His script is clear and elegant, stunning in its clarity, as though George Herman Ruth somehow knew that the artifact he was creating would survive so many centuries beyond his time on the Earth.

Barry Halper, Yankee collector extraordinaire who is profiled in Chapter 13, had a hand in the "Great Babe Ruth Revival" in September of 1999. It wasn't that hobby reverence for Ruth had diminished, merely that the full extent of it – its scale and intensity – wasn't clearly understood up to that point. The seven-day auction of Halper's collection from September 23-29 told the wider world what the top-rung of sports memorabilia collectors had always known: Just as it was in the American League in the 1920s, there was no one even close to The Bambino.

"Ruth was the man of the 20th century," Halper told the author from a skybox overlooking the Sotheby's auction floor before the hammer fell on the first of almost 2,500 lots. The gasps that roiled around the room for the next week obviously weren't all courtesy of

Ruth, but some of the biggest ones certainly were.

The contract that sold him from the Red Sox to the Yankees sold for $189,500; the bat that he leaned on in that stunning 1948 Pulitzer Prize-winning photo of his farewell at Yankee Stadium went for $107,000. The bat, actually Hall-of-Fame pitcher Bob Feller's own lumber that was handed to Ruth to steady himself that day, was purchased by the Upper Deck Co., makers of modern baseball cards and later featured to good effect in a sweepstakes sales promotion.

Over the course of that week, eager collectors would purchase Babe's glove ($121,000), a home uniform ($79,500), his rookie card ($79,500), his last game-used bat ($74,000) and even his player contract from 1933 and 1934, among others ($63,000 each). In a sale that totaled up more than $22 million in one week, The Sultan of Swat could lay claim to having knocked in as much or more of that total than anyone else.

The contract that sent Ruth from Boston to New York would sell six years later for $996,000 at Sotheby's/SCP; the famed auction

Perez-Steele Hall
of Fame Postcard,
single-signed Ruth
ball and 1933 Goudey
Ruth No. 181.

Babe Ruth by Andy Jurinko.

houses would also sell Ruth's 1923 bat used to hit the first home run at Yankee Stadium on April 18, 1923. That remarkable piece of lumber would bring $1.26 million, making it one of a handful of memorabilia items to have surpassed that particular threshold.

And though the Babe Ruth Story was never really about money – though he made and needed to make a great deal of it throughout his lifetime – keeping his eye on the finances did figure in one of those mythic moments at the height of his career.

At the height of the Depression, when told accusingly that his $80,000 salary was more than President Herbert Hoover's, Ruth is said to have deadpanned, "Yeah, but I had a better year than he did."

And the Babe's outdistanced everybody else – except maybe Elvis – in the afterlife, too.

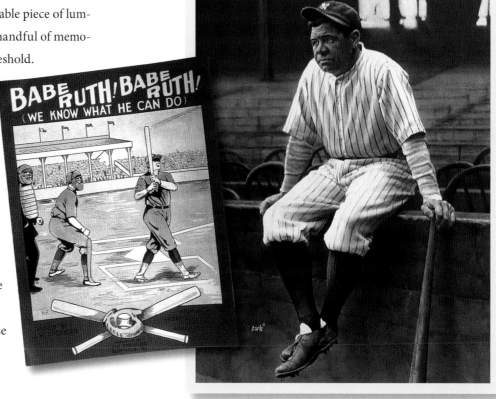

Babe Ruth art (above and lower left) by Ron Stark; Ruth sheet music, photos and bust on facing page from the David Spindel Collection.

Items from the Barry Halper Collection are shown above and at right.

"Lou Gehrig" by Ron Stark.   www.ronstarkstudios.com

Chapter 4

Gehrig

"*This is the story of a hero of the peaceful paths of everyday life,*" *the voice-over intones solemnly at the beginning of "The Pride of the Yankees," the 1942 feature film about the life and death of Henry Louis Gehrig. The elegant eulogy belonged to Damon Runyon; the man being eulogized belonged to the whole country.*

"*He faced death with that same valor and fortitude that has been displayed by thousands of young Americans on far-flung fields of battle,*" *the narrator continued. "He left behind him a memory of courage and devotion that will ever be an inspiration to all men. This is the story of Lou Gehrig.*"

When the critically acclaimed film opened on July 14, 1942, the United States was early into World War II, with a grateful nation fully understanding the linkage between a gifted, graceful athlete cruelly struck down in his prime and the deaths that awaited their fathers, sons and brothers in the European and Pacific Theatres. The story of Gehrig's life would have resonated at any time, but his death a year earlier in the middle of global conflagration made the story all the more compelling. This was many years before the first television commentator (no televisions!) would mumble anything about "American values," but few athletes ever more completely embodied everything that the average American male would ever want to be.

Gary Cooper as "The Iron Horse."

That said, the luckiest man on the face of the Earth didn't really seem all that lucky for the bulk of his major-league career or in the tragic death that struck him down late in his career but still at the young age of 37.

Gehrig, who would ultimately be voted the greatest first baseman in the history of the game, spent much of his remarkable career overshadowed by the only ballplayer on the planet capable of seeming larger and more compelling than he was: Babe Ruth.

Of course, it was hardly unlucky to have had Babe for a teammate for a dozen years, since the combination of the two helped propel the Yankees to four pennants and three World Series titles. But it also took a player who would have been the marquee name on any team and made him the second banana, despite producing offensively at a level that was unheard of in the game. Unheard of, that is, except for Babe Ruth.

When Ruth signed for 1935 with the Boston Braves, the spotlight finally shifted to Gehrig, who was coming off his Triple Crown season of 49 home runs, 165 RBI, and a .363 batting average. Gehrig would have exactly one season – and an off year, at that – to be atop the marquee alone. By 1936, a 21-year-old Joe DiMaggio showed up at Yankee Stadium by way of the Pacific Coast League, and pretty quickly was the center of attention from eager fans and a voracious Yankee press corps.

Felled by the disease that would ultimately bear his name, amyotrophic lateral sclerosis (ALS), Gehrig would miss milestones that almost certainly would have easily fallen his way. Though nobody made much of a fuss about it at the time, he missed the 500 Home Run Club by just seven dingers, and had he played another season and one half he would have compiled 3,000 hits.

His self-enforced removal from a game against the Tigers at Briggs Stadium on April 30, 1939, also had the effect of halting a pretty significant number: 2,130. As in consecutive games. Like Ruth's No. 714, it was one of the most well-known numbers in all of

1981 Sporting News Conlon Collection card (top) and original artwork of Gehrig by Ron Stark.

"Lou Gehrig's Farewell to Baseball" by Arthur K. Miller   www.artofthegame.com

Being a spokesman for a cigarette brand didn't carry the stigma in the 1930s that it does these days.

baseball, a title weakened not at all by the fact that another Hall of Famer would eclipse the mark many generations in the future.

It was a cruel irony that a man who should have first been remembered for the quality of his work was instead most prominently remembered for showing up for it. Which is not to suggest that fans overlooked his home runs or his .340 lifetime batting mark or his Herculean RBI production, but merely to acknowledge that the idiosyncratic numbers sometime can take on a life of their own.

There's so much about Gehrig that would have been startling all by itself, but taken in conjunction with his placement alongside Babe Ruth on perhaps the greatest team of all time makes it all the more noteworthy. For example, in 1927 he knocked in 175 runs in a season when the guy batting in front of him knocked in 164 and hit 60 home runs. While it helps to have a Babe Ruth batting in front of you in the order, it also means that a full 104 opportunities to drive

in runs have been removed.

For a statistic so dependent upon having an adequate number of chances, Gehrig's almost unmatched run production takes on additional import. He knocked in more than 140 runs eight different times, and just to balance it out, scored more than 130 runs in a season nine times.

Throughout the course of the 10 full seasons that Ruth and Gehrig combined to form perhaps the greatest 1-2 punch ever, it was Lou's consistency that neatly complemented Ruth's meteoric flashes. Over the course of that span, Ruth hit more home runs, but The Iron Horse had more RBIs, 120 more to be exact, a great season's worth for the sluggers of today. Over that 10-year span, playing the 154-game schedule, Gehrig averaged about 140 RBIs, per season; Ruth about 130.

Gehrig had other things to hang his hat on in the informal competition with his flamboyant teammate. One that comes quickly to mind is the extraordinary record of topping the 400 total bases threshold five different times. Like Gehrig himself, it's a kind of unsexy distinction, but one that true baseball fans recognize as reflective of a level of power and consistency rarely attained even by the greatest players.

Ruth, for example managed it only twice, including 417 in that awe-inspiring 1927 season when the Babe wound up with the 60 home runs, but his younger teammate piled up 447 total bases, the highest such mark since Ruth had managed 457 in his 59-homer 1921 season.

Gehrig also socked four home runs in a game, nailed down a Triple Crown, and was one of two players – along with Stan Musial – to compile 500 doubles, 150 triples and 400 home runs in a career. That's the kind of stuff that piles up total bases.

More poignantly, his 1939 farewell speech at Yankee Stadium ranks as one of the greatest moments in baseball history, revered by generations of fans, many of whom may actually have been thinking of Gary Cooper when Gehrig's name was mentioned, but who

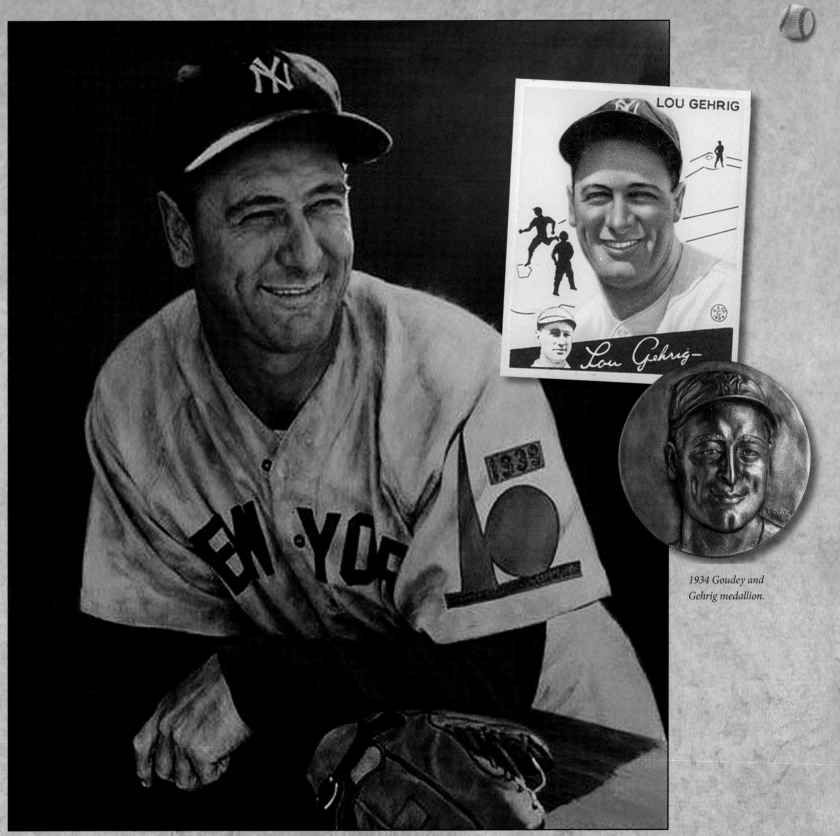

Lou Gehrig artwork by Ron Stark.

1934 Goudey and
Gehrig medallion.

LOU GEHRIG

understood all that the ballplayer represented nonetheless.

That Gehrig's story was further enhanced by Hollywood did nothing but expand the mythology that would ultimately be attached to the man. The movie, which would be sneered at in modern times by youngsters weaned on computers and video games, was heralded as a classic by moviegoers in 1942, and promptly rewarded with 11 Oscar nominations, and an eventual win for film editing.

Collectors Corner: Lou Gehrig memorabilia in general – and his signature in particular – can be far rarer than Ruth material, but The Bambino still overshadows in price on much of it despite the fact that more Ruth items survived.

But at the biggest auction of the last millennium, the sale of the famed Barry Halper Collection in September of 1999 at Sotheby's in New York City, Lou topped his old teammate with some gusto. In an historic seven-day sale that helped put sports memorabilia collecting in the big time, the first baseman's glove from Gehrig's final game and a 1927 Gehrig road jersey would sell for $387,500 and $305,000, respectively, absolutely startling dollar amounts in 1999. The escalation of highest-tier memorabilia pricing over the last decade would almost certainly leave both items in seven figures were they to face the auction block in 2008. Just for good measure, Gehrig's cap from the 1930s ($151,000) and his 1927 World Series ring ($96,000) would make for a nice four-bagger at the $22-million sale.

Though the Sultan of Swat wound up holding a similar title in the arcane world of baseball memorabilia, it was Gehrig who was the first athlete to ever appear on a Wheaties box, a kind of informal anointing in the middle of the Depression that here was the great star of the Yankees, humble, taciturn, seemingly the perfect pitchman to entice millions of youngsters to eat their breakfast cereal. Sadly, he was also the first athlete to have his number retired at the same July 4, 1939, farewell at the Stadium.

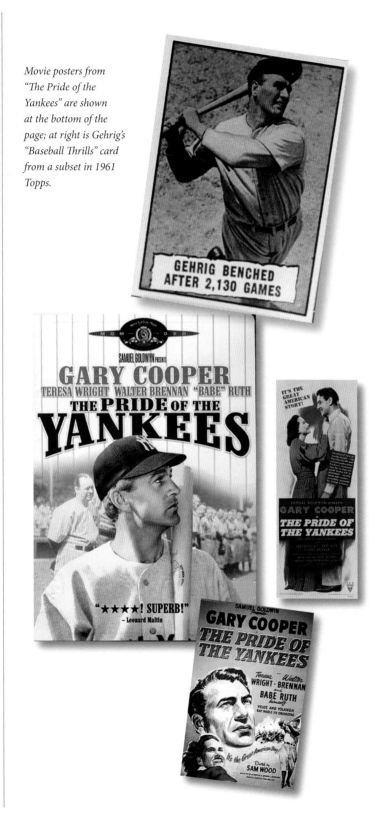

Movie posters from "The Pride of the Yankees" are shown at the bottom of the page; at right is Gehrig's "Baseball Thrills" card from a subset in 1961 Topps.

Ruth and Gehrig original art by Ron Stark www.ronstarkstudios.com;
plus hand-painted Gehrig baseball by Monty Sheldon. www.montysheldon.com.

"Joe DiMaggio" by Darryl Vlasak.

Chapter 5

Joe DiMaggio

"Joe, you never heard such cheering," Marilyn Monroe said to her new husband, Joe DiMaggio, upon returning from a side trip during their honeymoon in 1954 where she had visited American troops in South Korea. "Yes, I have," Joe replied.

And, indeed, Joe DiMaggio had heard the cheers to a degree that few athletes can ever imagine. His unique status as an iconic American hero so completely transcended the world of sports that he was heralded in literature, song and poetry, though not all of it was as exemplary as the man.

Still, when Hemingway's old Cuban fisherman Santiago tells his apprentice about "the Great DiMaggio," there's an exalted reverence for a mere ballplayer, an intimation from the The Old Man and the Sea's protagonist that DiMaggio's exploits ranged far beyond the confines of Yankee Stadium's vast center field. Like his predecessor at the throne of Major League Baseball, Babe Ruth, DiMaggio parlayed extraordinary diamond skills with a flair for the dramatic and a demeanor that bespoke of an imperious elegance. Of such concoctions are deities made.

Oct. 10, 1939 Look magazine.

This was the hold that DiMaggio had on millions in the years from the end of the Great Depression to the beginning of the Korean War.

The myth of The Yankee Clipper is as resounding and compelling as the man, but the myth suffers in comparison because it confines itself to the constraints of the heroic, the banality of a perceived perfection. While the incessant polishing and protection of the image was a hallmark of much of the man's story – virtually from his earliest days as a Pacific Coast League sensation for the San Francisco Seals to his second career atop the baseball memorabilia world – it belied a man riddled with contradictions.

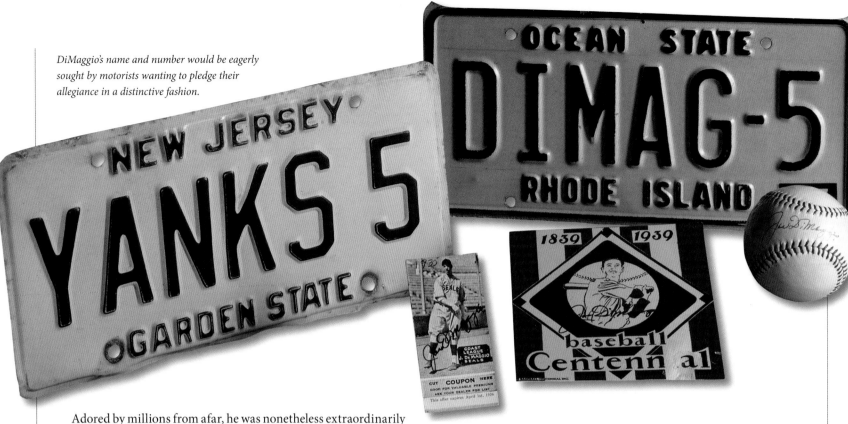

DiMaggio's name and number would be eagerly sought by motorists wanting to pledge their allegiance in a distinctive fashion.

Adored by millions from afar, he was nonetheless extraordinarily alone, a man apart from even those closest to him, ultimately largely incapable of the kind of spontaneous, unstudied affection that was lavished on him by so many. Obsessed with his storied legend, he did many small, petty things ostensibly to safeguard the larger ones, the mixture of the real and the mythical. Already an idol to so many as he hobbled away from the Yankees after the 1951 World Series, he took yet another step to boost his other-worldly ranking; he married the most beautiful woman in the universe. The marriage would last only months; the legacy of the biggest name in sports exchanging vows with Hollywood's reigning sex symbol will last forever.

Yankee Stadium was his home, an edifice as steeped in baseball lore and legend as the man himself, but it was also his nemesis. "The House That Ruth Built" certainly wasn't a bit of architecture with the righty swinging DiMaggio in mind. The vast left field and centerfield dimensions devoured many an extra-base hit and even home runs from the great star, leading to more musings from his loyalists about what the batting average might have been had he played in the Beantown bandbox of his archrival Red Sox.

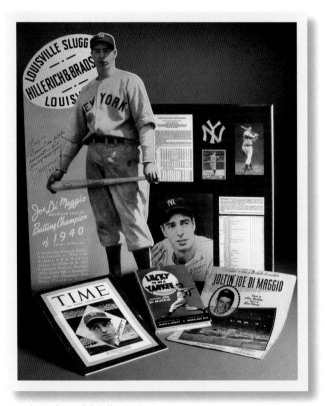

(David Spindel Collection)

Perhaps the greatest contradiction is rarely discussed, and certainly not within circles that revere the man. The Herculean status accorded DiMaggio came about from the combination of his own persona and his cosmic placement on a ball club that he would lead to 10 AL pennants and nine World Series titles over his career. Thus the overriding point of the entire enterprise, winning baseball games, became synonymous with his name, and yet for many fans he's remembered more for the baseball parlor trick of hitting in 56 consecutive games. How's that for irony: revered on the one hand as the quintessential winner of his or any generation, he nonetheless gained even more fame from a peculiar baseball statistical contrivance that doesn't necessarily further that noble end all that much.

If the silly streak has overshadowed much of his amazing accomplishments these days, it didn't at all back then. The Yankee Clipper wound up socking 361 home runs playing half of his games in that aforementioned Stadium, batted .325 lifetime and just barely recorded more strikeouts than homers (369-361). His war-shortened career kept his lifetime numbers from threatening those of so many of his fellow Hall of Famers, but the aura of DiMaggio is infinitely broader than any rote interpretation of statistics. Winning was what the game was all about, and winning was what he did.

That penchant for coming out atop the standings left Joe peculiarly advantaged when it came time for the voting on more subjective awards, in this instance most notably the Most Valuable Player Award. His unparalleled position as the marquee player on the best team in baseball helped propel him to three MVPs, which is not too shabby for a guy who missed the prime years from age 28-30.

But again, it was hardly the numbers that gave life to DiMaggio lore. He was regarded almost from the start as perhaps the most graceful player to have ever played the game, a universally held but informal designation that he guarded as carefully as any other facet of his persona.

DiMaggio was a favorite of magazine and book publishers, showing up in everything from children's books and comics, mainstream news magazines and even sheet music. Also shown, a DiMaggio jersey and bronze statue.
(David Spindel Collection)

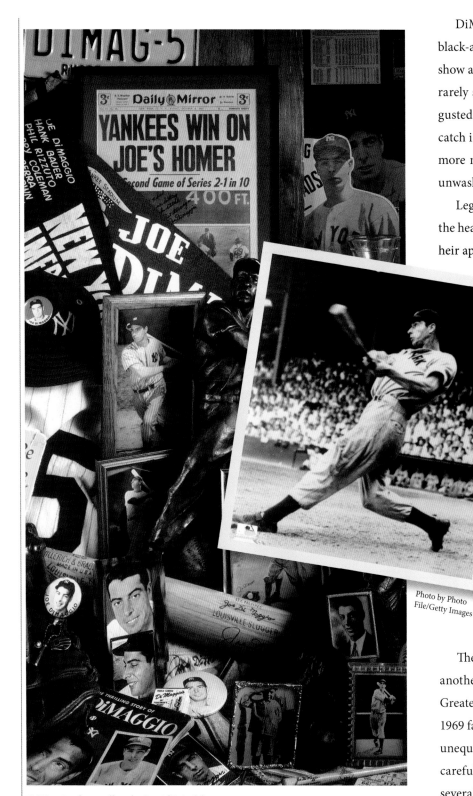

DiMaggio lives for most fans in wartime newsreel footage, grainy black-and-white testimonials to his greatness, flickering frames that show a long graceful swing and a studied, almost stoic manner that rarely showed a glimmer of emotion. With that backdrop, his disgusted booting of second base after Al Gionfriddo's game-saving catch in the 1947 World Series of Joe's 415-foot blast became all the more noteworthy. The Great DiMaggio didn't like to let the great unwashed get a peek at the human side of their hero.

Legend has it that the preoccupation with not looking bad was at the heart of the 1951 World Series play that would severely injure his heir apparent, Mickey Mantle. As the duo converged on a fly ball in Game 2, the story goes that Joe pulled up on the ball out of fear of looking awkward, and Mickey, charging to make the play, turned his knee on a drainage pipe, tearing cartilage and ending his first World Series. Those details of that famous fly ball are attributed to Mantle himself, though they certainly are second or maybe third hand.

Marty Appel, the noted author and public relations specialist who was the Yankees' PR maven through much of the 1970s, provides his own recollection of Joe's insistence on presenting only a carefully crafted image to his fans. Appel tells of a Cracker Jack Old-Timer's Game in the 1980s when Joe was changing into his uniform shirt and a photographer snapped a picture of a still-fit but hardly Adonis-like retired athlete. DiMaggio angrily told him to stop shooting – and never again allowed that kind of unguarded moment to take place.

The man with so many decidedly cool and regal nicknames had another title that he treasured as much as any of them. "America's Greatest Living Player" was a designation accorded him in a famous 1969 fan ballot marking baseball's centennial, and Joe reveled in the unequivocal nature of it. Ultimately, it would become part of the carefully scripted presentation of the post-retirement DiMaggio. For several generations of fans, it would be taken as an article of faith.

Photo by Photo File/Getty Images

DiMaggio photo collage by David Spindel; www.spindelvisions.com.

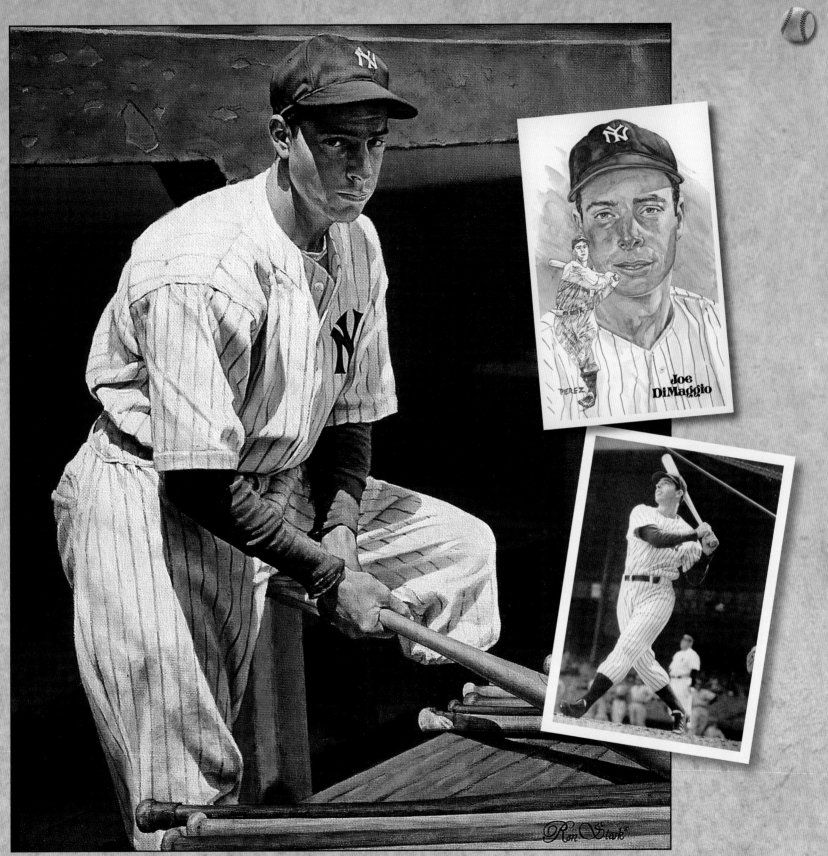

Joe DiMaggio artwork by Ron Stark.   www.ronstarkstudios.com

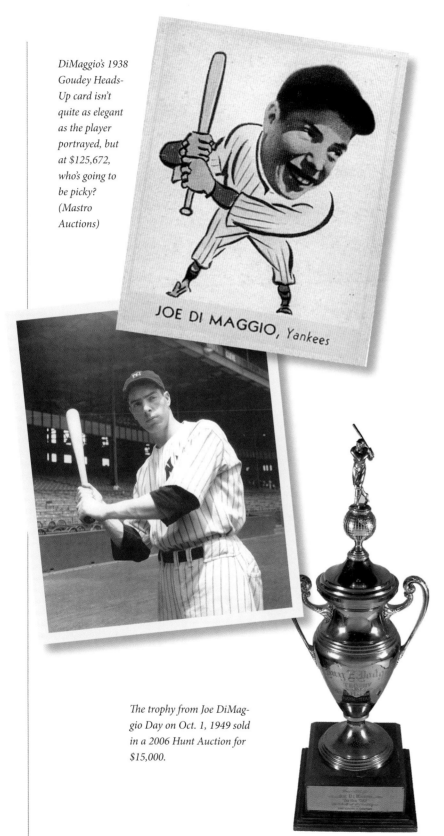

DiMaggio's 1938 Goudey Heads-Up card isn't quite as elegant as the player portrayed, but at $125,672, who's going to be picky? (Mastro Auctions)

The trophy from Joe DiMaggio Day on Oct. 1, 1949 sold in a 2006 Hunt Auction for $15,000.

DiMaggio's time center stage at Yankee Stadium was relatively short: from his stunning rookie season in 1936 and a meteoric ascension to the most famous player in the game to his retirement following that injury-plagued 1951 season, it would be only 16 years, with three of those lost to the same world war that helped to forge the DiMaggio legend. In only 13 seasons, he kept alive the chain of the most spectacular multi-generation dynasty in the history of professional sports, one that dated back to Ruth's first homer at Yankee Stadium in 1923 to the mid-1960s when the clock finally ran out on Yankees dominance. By then, Joe DiMaggio had started to fade from the national consciousness just a wee bit, leading eventually to Paul Simon's asking lyrically, "Where have you gone, Joe DiMaggio?"

He hadn't really gone much of anywhere, but he was about to return to center stage as the nostalgia that helped power so much of the DiMaggio mystique was about to be directed on to another stage ... one perfectly suited to the regal imprimatur of one Joseph Paul DiMaggio.

Sometime in the 1970s, a small army of peripatetic baseball card dealers made a good deal of noise as they roamed around the countryside renting rooms at the local Holiday Inns. With small notices in local newspapers, they oddly announced that they would pay genuine U.S. currency for your old baseball cards. It would become the stuff of thousands of headlines: Cardboard Gold, Treasure in the Attic, that sort of thing. The cliched pronouncement that baseball card collectors had "come out of the closet" would eventually have to be discarded as the phrase took on a more culturally significant meaning. However you described it, the nostalgia of the Golden Era of postwar Major League Baseball had launched itself on a bewildered American public.

How better to cope with such an unnerving turn of events than for the nation to turn its eyes to Mr. DiMaggio, retired nearly three decades now and shilling for a gadget as all-American as he was: a coffee maker. Mr. Coffee, as a whole generation of citizens had grown to know him, was about to get his old nicknames back with a vengeance.

❖

"There are 250 million Americans, and each and every one should own a Joe DiMaggio signed baseball." So said a prominent baseball card dealer who knew well of Joltin' Joe's legendary abilities at baseball card shows. Once the organized baseball card hobby started picking up steam in the 1980s, DiMaggio was front and center as show promoters eventually realized that bringing back retired ballplayers to sign autographs was a surefire way to activate that nostalgia gene that seemed embedded in so many.

Modern fans and collectors know that DiMaggio-signed baseballs can be had from that glossy catalog in the seat pocket of the passenger directly in front of you on your flight from Atlanta to Columbus, but not everybody recalls that the signature wasn't always that expensive. As late as 1991, DiMaggio was signing at card shows for a measly $25 per signature, but all that changed when Joe signed a contract with the now-defunct Score Board Co., reportedly earning $3.5 million to sign literally thousands of items for the Cherry Hill, N.J.-based firm.

Just as he had with his $100,000 salary at the peak of his playing career, he quickly "lifted all boats" with his huge paychecks on the autograph circuit, ultimately matching his top baseball salary with a day or two of carefully signing his famous name.

Top of page: Assorted DiMaggio memorabilia courtesy of the David Spindel Collection.

1938 Yankees
Photo courtesy of Hunt Auctions

From left, Hunt Auctions photo, DiMaggio signs autographs, and Andy Jurinko artwork.

Card dealers told of signing sessions where DiMaggio would sign his name between 1,000 and 1,500 times in a single afternoon. His signature is as careful, guarded and elegant as everything else that he deemed of importance in his life, and indeed, he reportedly understood to a great degree the impact that a simple signature could have on a shiny new official baseball or a glossy black-and-white 8-by-10 photograph.

The story goes that a friend was visiting DiMaggio at his San Francisco home in the early 1980s when the man noticed that DiMaggio's sister, Marie, who lived with Joe, was signing some of the requests that had come in through the mail. When the friend explained to DiMaggio the significance for collectors in getting his actual signature, the ghost signing reportedly came to a halt.

As word of that spread through the then relatively narrow confines of the fledgling autograph hobby, DiMaggio's weekly mail volume promptly exploded to the point that he would no longer sign through the mail. The show schedule quickly picked up in a big way.

It was in this colorful, chaotic world of sports memorabilia collectors that DiMaggio would befriend, and later reject – for a time – the man who would help build the sports memorabilia hobby into the behemoth that it has become today.

Barry Halper, profiled in another chapter of this book, was one of Joe's biggest fans, a part-owner of the Yankees and by the 1980s already entrenched as the most prolific baseball memorabilia collector in the world. In Halper's famous basement of his Livingston, N.J., home, he had literally hundreds of pieces connected to DiMaggio, and over the span of nearly two decades, the Hall of Famer would visit this informal hall of fame and quite literally sign his way from room to room.

On one occasion in the early 1990s, after DiMaggio had been visiting Halper's home for more than 10 years, the collector cautiously pulled out an original copy of "Playboy" magazine, the first issue and the one featuring Marilyn Monroe on the cover.

File photos of autographed DiMaggio memorabilia.

"What do you want me to do, sign it?" DiMaggio asked sharply. Halper sheepishly nodded yes, and, to his surprise, Joe did end up signing it, but with a pretty significant caveat: no one would ever see it as long as DiMaggio was alive.

And, of course, his friend honored the stipulation. The author can vouch for that as well: Halper wouldn't even offer a peek during a lengthy visit to his suburban New Jersey home in 1996 for an extensive article for *Sports Collectors Digest* magazine. DiMaggio died on March 8, 1999; the bulk of the Halper Collection, including the copy of "Playboy," was sold by Sotheby's in September of the same year. The magazine ended up selling for just over $40,000.

The Yankee Clipper was front and center – or his autograph was – three weeks after the last item was sold in the Halper Auction. On October 13, a reported 400 federal agents fanned out across five states to stage coordinated morning raids on 60 homes and businesses, sacking the most prolific and profitable forgery rings in the history of crime in America.

Of the estimated $10 million in seized goods, Joe DiMaggio items were among the most frequently forged. Not surprisingly, it would shake the very foundations of the autograph business for years to come, but it speaks to the power of a Yankee Clipper autograph that 10 years later it has withstood the turmoil and remains one of the priciest of all postwar deceased players. Ironically, the forgers created a further abomination by abetting the scam by creating bogus letters of authenticity that carried the signature of a "J. DiMaggio," obviously no relation.

And in a further irony, the man who earned many millions of dollars more for signing his name than he ever did for playing the game batted .500 with a couple of his own autograph requests.

According to Marty Appel, DiMaggio managed to get a baseball

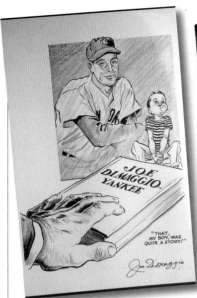

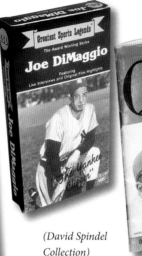

(David Spindel
Collection)

Still, a remarkable 1938 Goudey Heads-Up card from the famed Lionel Carter Collection sold for $125,672 in a Mastro Auction in 2006, and a number of other DiMaggio cards in top condition have sold for upwards of $20,000-$30,000 in recent years.

With the break in baseball card production during World War II, there was nothing of the most-famous baseball player in America for wartime youth to collect, and scant little after it was over. DiMaggio appears in the 1948 Leaf set, but mysteriously is never included in the earliest card sets produced by a pair of fledgling companies: Topps and Bowman. He never had a contract with Bowman and thus never appeared in the classic sets produced by that company from 1948-51, nor did he show up in the campy Red and Blue Back Topps sets of 1951. Curiously, he did have a card in the odd little Berk Ross issue in 1952, the year following his final season.

The lack of cardboard chops had no impact, however, on his memorabilia, which has always been among the most coveted. DiMaggio's last Most Valuable Player trophy from 1947 sold in a Hunt Auction in 2006 for $281,750, the same special sale that included his final World Series uniform from 1951 ($195,500), his 1951 road jersey ($166,750) and Marilyn Monroe's 1954 passport from her Far East tour with Joe that year. A Monroe-signed photo with the inscription "I love you, Joe" sold for $80,500 in that May 2006 auction.

For maybe the only time in her life, Marilyn was not alone on this one.

signed by Ronald Reagan and Mikhail Gorbachev in 1988, then swung and missed at getting another world figure to sign a couple of years later.

NBC correspondent Andrea Mitchell told in her 2005 book *Talking Back .... to Presidents, Dictators, and Assorted Scoundrels* of a visit by the Queen of England to Baltimore's old Memorial Stadium in 1991. DiMaggio was among the notables invited to mingle with The Queen, and he reportedly took a baseball out of his jacket and handed it to one of the Queen's flunkies (our word, not hers), asking if she would sign.

As the story goes, the request was passed along, but the ball made it's way back to Joe in an unsigned state. "The Queen does not sign baseballs," he was told icily.

So much for professional courtesy among royalty.

Collectors Corner: It is a function of nothing more than the period that Joe DiMaggio played, from 1936-51, that his impact in the card-collecting arena is relatively shortchanged. Joe arrived in Gotham as the country still struggled with the Depression, and yet was too late to be included in arguably the top baseball card sets from the decade, the Goudey and Diamond Star issues.

*Marilyn Monroe photo from
the DiMaggio Collection.*
Hunt Auctions

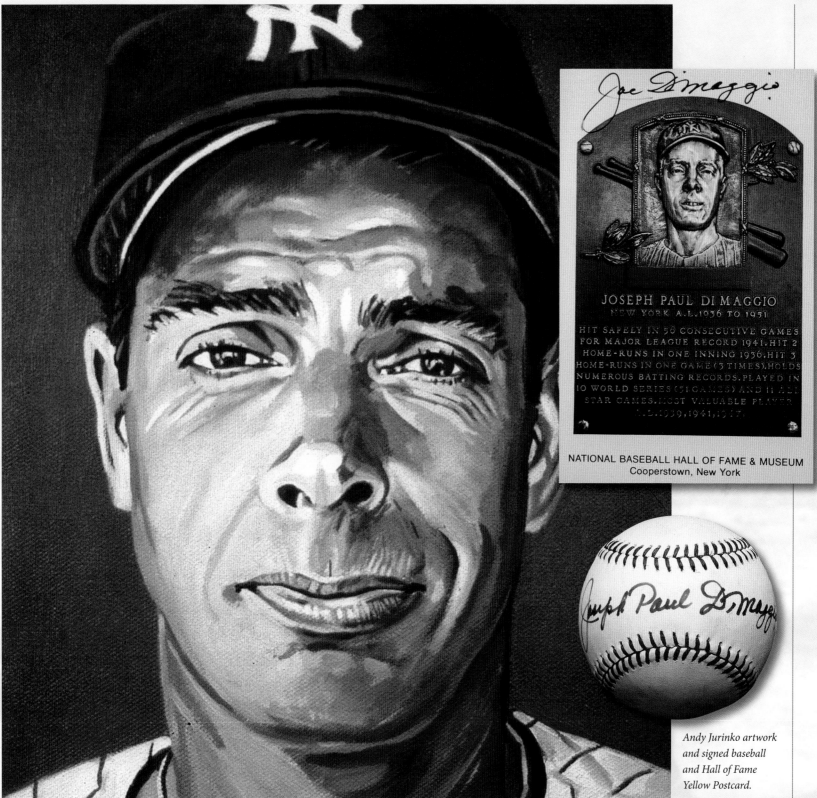

JOSEPH PAUL DI MAGGIO
NEW YORK A.L. 1936 TO 1951

HIT SAFELY IN 56 CONSECUTIVE GAMES
FOR MAJOR LEAGUE RECORD 1941. HIT 2
HOME-RUNS IN ONE INNING 1936. HIT 3
HOME-RUNS IN ONE GAME (3 TIMES). HOLDS
NUMEROUS BATTING RECORDS. PLAYED IN
10 WORLD SERIES (51 GAMES) AND 11 ALL
STAR GAMES. MOST VALUABLE PLAYER
A.L. 1939, 1941, 1947.

NATIONAL BASEBALL HALL OF FAME & MUSEUM
Cooperstown, New York

*Andy Jurinko artwork
and signed baseball
and Hall of Fame
Yellow Postcard.*

Fan waves an American flag during pre-game ceremonies honoring the first anniversary of the 9/11 terrorist attacks before the Yankees-Orioles game at Yankee Stadium Sept. 11, 2002.

Chapter 6

Stadium Photo Album

Yankees souvenir pennant.

Joe DiMaggio, circa 1945, still holding the bat after following through with a swing during a game.

Photo by Photo File/Getty Images

1941 Yankees scorecard.

Yankee Stadium bench seat.

1957 World Series program.

The 1957 World Series featured the Yankees against the Milwaukee Braves, led by NL MVP Hank Aaron. The Braves won the Series in seven games, behind Lew Burdette's three complete game victories, and became the first team to win a championship after relocating.

David Wells pitches in the top of the ninth inning on May 17, 1998. Wells pitched a perfect game by retiring all 27 batters he faced as the Yankees beat the Minnesota Twins 4-0.

MATT CAMPBELL/AFP/Getty Images

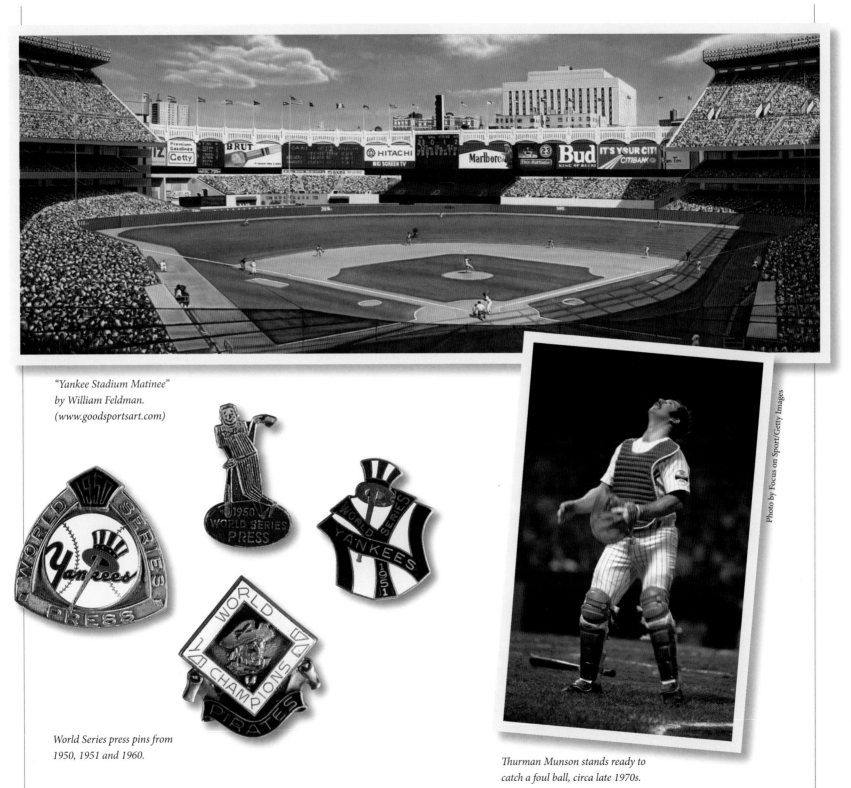

"Yankee Stadium Matinee"
by William Feldman.
(www.goodsportsart.com)

World Series press pins from
1950, 1951 and 1960.

Photo by Focus on Sport/Getty Images

Thurman Munson stands ready to
catch a foul ball, circa late 1970s.

Darryl Strawberry's 1996 World Series ring.
(Leland.com Auctions)

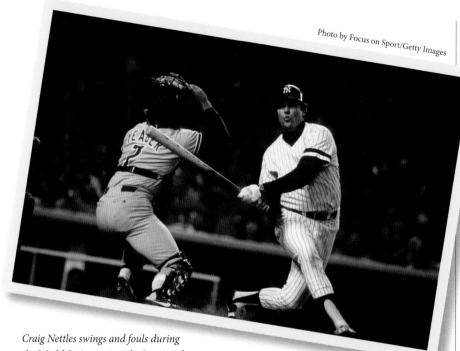

Photo by Focus on Sport/Getty Images

Craig Nettles swings and fouls during
the World Series against the Los Angeles
Dodgers in October 1981.

"Outside Yankee Stadium"
artwork by William Feldman.
www.goodsportsart.com

1981 World Series full
ticket. The 1981 World
Series saw the Yankees
fall to the Dodgers
in six games. The
Yankees would not
appear in a World
Series again for
15 years.

David Cone celebrates as his teammates lift him after pitching a perfect game against the Montreal Expos on July 18, 1999 as the Yankees defeated the Expos 6-0.

Ticket stub from Roger Maris' 61st home run game.

ENTER GATE 6
(OR NEAREST OPEN GATE)

19	317A	7
SEC.	BOX	SEAT

| 81 | SUN. OCT. — 1961 — | 1 |

LOWER BOX SEAT $3.50

RAIN CHECK

ADMIT ONE • Subject to the conditions set forth on the back hereof. 82

SECOND RAIN CHECK
In the event of a postponement this contest and entitle the holder to the game numbered hereon. Not good if detached from Original Rain Check.

GAME NO. 81

General view of the field during an interleague game between the Yankees and New York Mets on June 18, 1997. The Yankees won 3-2.

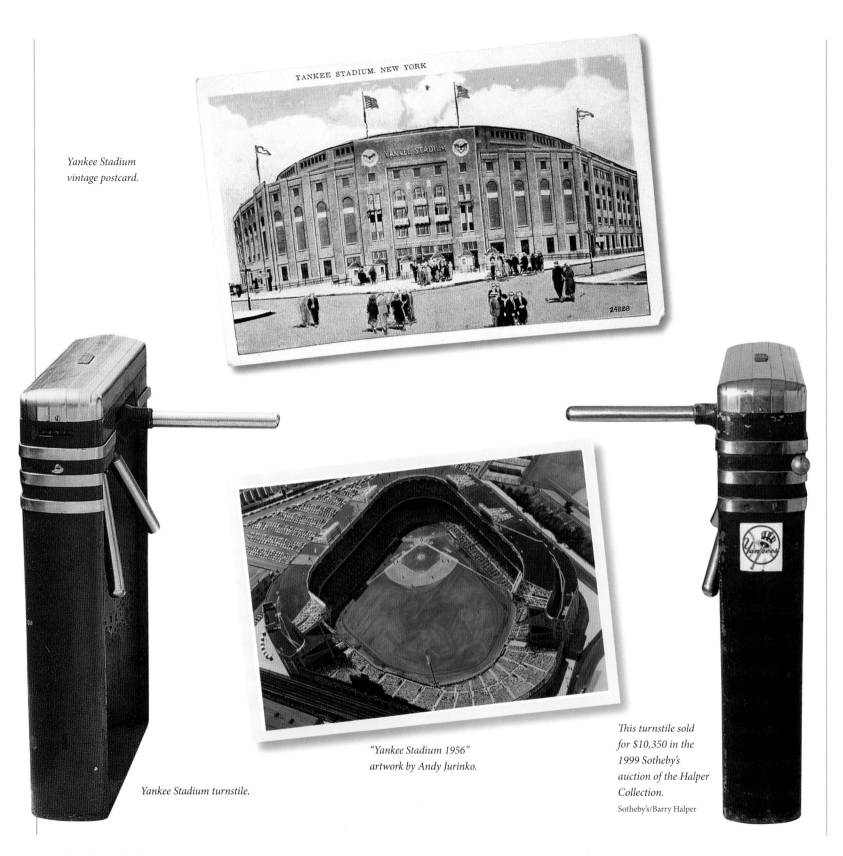

Yankee Stadium vintage postcard.

Yankee Stadium turnstile.

"Yankee Stadium 1956" artwork by Andy Jurinko.

This turnstile sold for $10,350 in the 1999 Sotheby's auction of the Halper Collection.

Sotheby's/Barry Halper

Babe Ruth and Lou Gehrig signed ball.

Robert Edward Auctions photo

Yankee Stadium seat.

Photo by B Bennett/Getty Images

Lou Gehrig leaps straight into the air to make a catch, early 1930s.

The baseball that Mickey Mantle struck for home run No. 16 in the World Series in 1964 sold for $80,000 in the December 2008 Mastro Auction.

*Yankee World Series press pins from
1950, 1952, 1953 and 1955.*

*Outfielders Roger Maris (left) and Mickey Mantle (right) flank Willie Mays of the San Francisco Giants prior to
the Major League Baseball All-Star Game on July 13, 1960 at Yankee Stadium. The National League defeated the
American League, 6-0, as Mays added a home run.*

*In 2008, Upper Deck made a set of 6,500 cards called "Yankee Stadium Legacy."
It is the largest set of baseball cards ever produced.*

photo courtesy of Upper Deck

Del Webb's Yankees World Series ring collection sold for
$310,500 at the 1999 Sotheby's Barry Halper Collection auction.

Sotheby's/Barry Halper

Bleacher ticket
stub from the
1923 World
Series.

HENRY RAY ABRAMS/AFP/Getty Images

Mets' Luis Lopez (right) narrowly beats the pick-off throw from Andy Pettitte to Tino Martinez (left)
in the second inning of the first interleague game at Yankee Stadium between the New York teams
on June 16, 1997.

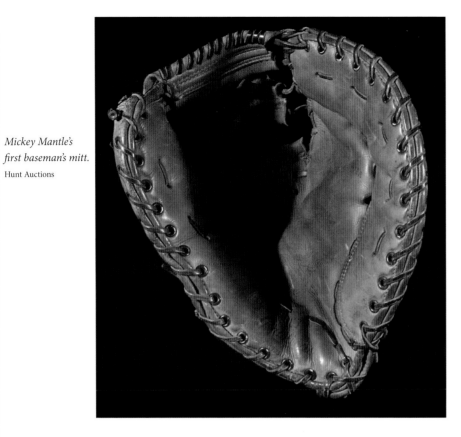

Mickey Mantle's first baseman's mitt.
Hunt Auctions

Babe Ruth, playing right field, backs up for a fly ball. From May 18, 1921.

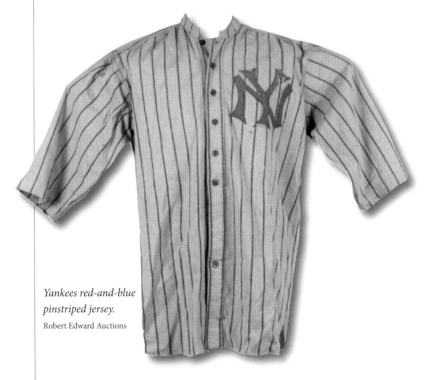

Yankees red-and-blue pinstriped jersey.
Robert Edward Auctions

Circa 1920s-30s Babe Ruth cap sold for $327,750 in the 2008 Hunt All-Star Auction in New York.

Photo Mark Rucker/Transcendental graphics/Getty Images

Gil McDougald takes the throw from Yogi Berra to put out sliding Gil Hodges, Dodger first baseman, at third base in inning eight of game one of the World Series on Sept. 30, 1953.

Ruth's plaque in Monument Park.

Full ticket from 1952 World Series.
The 1952 World Series featured the three-time defending champion Yankees beating the Brooklyn Dodgers in seven games. The Yankees won their fourth straight title—tying the mark they set between 1936 and 1939 under manager Joe McCarthy. Casey Stengel became the second manager in Major League history with four consecutive championships. It was the 15th championship in the Yankees' history, and the third defeat of the Dodgers in six years.

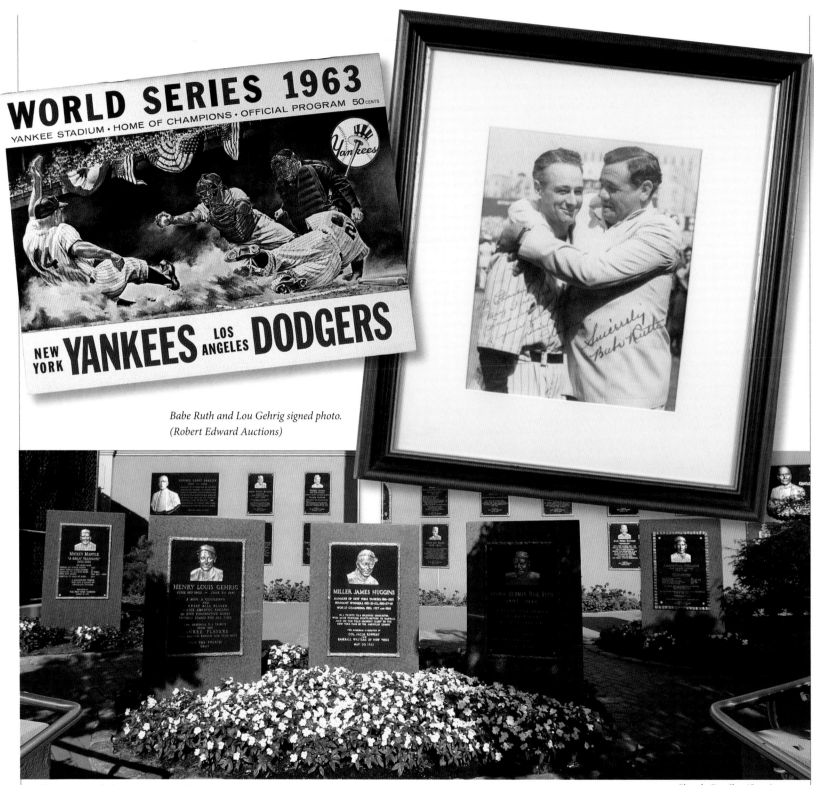

Babe Ruth and Lou Gehrig signed photo.
(Robert Edward Auctions)

The ceremonial plaques at the Stadium's Monument Park. Players consider receipt of a ceremonial plaque in Monument Park to be a
supreme distinction. The ceremonial monuments themselves are the highest honor of all, and are awarded posthumously.

Photo by Ezra Shaw/Getty Images

Ezra Shaw/ALLSPORT

1996 World Series ring presented to Phil Rizzuto.
(Geppi's Memorabilia Road Show)

Tino Martinez takes a curtain call after hitting a two-run home run in the 9th inning to tie the
Arizona Diamondbacks during game four of the World Series. The Yankees won 4-3.

Lou Gehrig's warm-up jacket dated to the final game of
his consecutive games streak in 1939 brought $373,750
in the 2008 Hunt All-Star Auction in New York.

The scoreboard in center field reads all zeros for the Minnesota Twins at the end of the game after pitcher David Wells threw a perfect game on May 17, 1998. Wells retired all 27 batters he faced as the Yankees beat the Twins 4-0.

1964 World Series ticket stub. The 1964 World Series pitted the Yankees and the Cardinals, with the Cardinals prevailing in seven games. St. Louis won its seventh world championship, while the Yankees, who had appeared in 14 of 16 World Series since 1949, would not play in the Series again until 1976.

Shortstop Derek Jeter hits the ball during a playoff game against the Baltimore Orioles on Oct. 9, 1996 The Yankees won the game, 5-4.

Outside shot of Yankee Stadium, circa 1963.

Souvenir Pennant.

"Yankee Stadium, 1964" by Andy Jurinko.

Thurman Munson's 1977 World Series ring brought $143,750 in the 2008 Hunt All-Star Auction in New York.

General view of Yankee Stadium during game one of the 2006 ALDS between the Yankees and Detroit Tigers. The Yankees won 8-4.

Outfielder Reggie Jackson swings and watches the flight of his ball during a circa late 1970s game. Jackson played for the Yankees from 1977-81.

1960 World Series full ticket. The 1960 World Series featured the Yankees against the Pittsburgh Pirates. The Pirates won the Series in seven games. To date it is the only World Series that has ended in the seventh game in the bottom of the 9th inning with a home run.

Lefty Gomez, left, and Lou Gehrig, center, discuss the quirks of Yankee Stadium with Jimmy Foxx of the Boston Red Sox before the start of the 1939 All Star Game on July 11.

Photo by Mark Rucker/Transcendental Graphics/Getty Images

Lou Gehrig is battling ALS disease as his batting struggles continue during a pre-season game at Brooklyn on April 18, 1939. The Brooklyn catcher is Babe Phelps.

Photo by Bruce Bennett Studios/Getty Images

Two dozen Yankee tickets from May 25, 1973.

New York Governor Alfred E. Smith throws out the first pitch at Yankee Stadium prior to the game between the Yankees and Red Sox on April 19, 1923.

Vintage New York Yankees bobbin' head doll.

Souvenir pennants.

Photo by Al Bello/Getty Images

Aaron Boone hits the game-winning home run in the bottom of the 11th inning against the Red Sox during game seven of the American League Championship Series on Oct. 16, 2003.

General view from the upper deck of Yankee Stadium during a game between the Yankees and Mets on July 10, 2003.

Photo by Jerry Driendl/Getty Images

Photo by Ezra Shaw/Getty Images

Manager Joe Torre wipes his eyes during the pre-game ceremony before taking on the Baltimore Orioles on Sept. 11, 2002.

Photo by Ezra Shaw/Getty Images

Aaron Boone celebrates after hitting the game-winning home run in the bottom of the 11th inning against the Red Sox during game seven of the American League Championship Series on Oct. 16, 2003. The Yankees won 6-5, advancing them to the World Series.

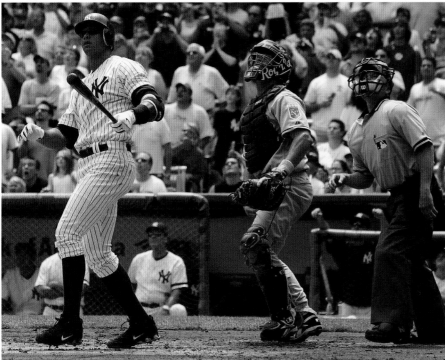

Pitcher Roger Clemens throws the broken bat of Mike Piazza of the New York Mets as Piazza runs to first base during the first inning of game two of the World Series on Oct. 22, 2000. The incident led to a dugout emptying confrontation between the two teams. Piazza's bat broke after hitting the ball and a piece of it flew in the direction of the mound. The Yankees won 6-5.

Alex Rodriguez watches the ball stay fair, along with home plate umpire Jerry Meals and catcher Jason LaRue of the Kansas City Royals, for his 500th career home run in the first inning against Kyle Davies on Aug. 4, 2007. The blast came on the first pitch he faced and was a three-run home run. Rodriguez became the 22nd player in history and youngest to hit 500 home runs.

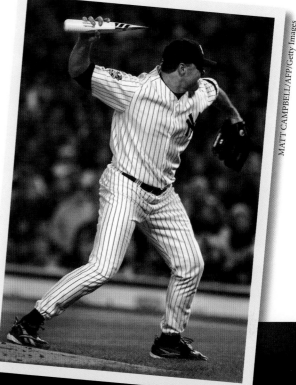

General view of Yankee Stadium taken before game one of the 2000 World Series on Oct. 21, 2000. The Yankees defeated the Mets 4-3 in 11 innings.

1963 World Series press pin.

LOU GEHRIG
MEMORIAL

JULY 4th, 1941

SECTION 27
BOX 2
SEAT 4

MEZZA STAND Est. Price $1.50
Reserved Seat Tax Paid .15
TOTAL $1.65

R-A-I-N C-H-E-C-K

"Yankee Shave" and Gehrig Memorial ticket stub
from the David Spindel Collection.

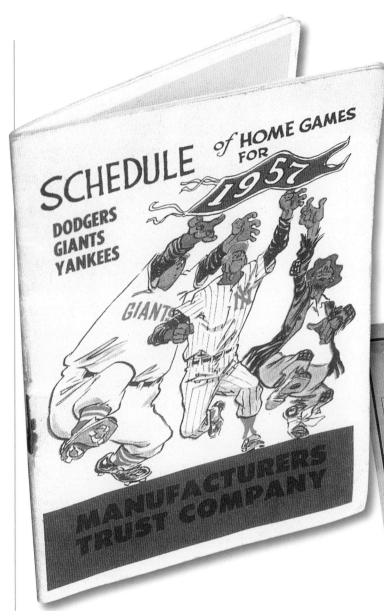

*Yankees, Dodgers and Giants Schedule Book for
1957 (upper left), 1955 Yankees Schedule (right)
and souvenir cigarette lighter (upper right).
(David Spindel Collection, www.spindelvisions.com)*

Hank Bauer autographed
photo (above), Greatest Sports
Moments LP (upper right) and
assorted bottle caps.
(David Spindel Collection,
www.spindelvisions.com)

MICKEY MANTLE

1st BASE

Ht.—6'0"   Wt: 201   Throws: Right   Bats: Both

NEW YORK YANKEES

Born: October 20, 1931   Home: Dallas, Texas

BASEBALL STAR CARD No. 2

★ ★ ★ ★ ★ ★ ★ ★ ★ ★

Elston Howard

NEW YORK YANKEES — CATCHER

Ht.—6'2"; Wt.—198; Bats—Right; Throws—Right
Born—February 23, 1929; Home—Teaneck, N. J.
Named the MVP in the International
League with Toronto, 1954, Elston
joined the Yankees in 1955. He received the Babe Ruth Award in 1958
for his outstanding play in the World
Series. A jack-of-all-trades with the
Yankees (filling in as outfielder,
catcher or pinch-hitter), he was selected for the 1960 All Star Game.

MAJOR LEAGUE BATTING RECORD

	Games	At Bat	Runs	Hits	2 B	3 B	HR	RBI	Avg.
1960	107	323	29	79	11	3	6	39	.245
LIFE	640	2,067	234	565	83	28	58	299	.270

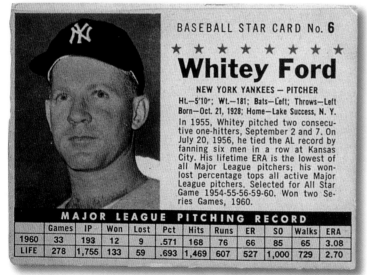

BASEBALL STAR CARD No. 6

★ ★ ★ ★ ★ ★ ★ ★ ★ ★

Whitey Ford

NEW YORK YANKEES — PITCHER

Ht.—5'10"; Wt.—181; Bats—Left; Throws—Left
Born—Oct. 21, 1928; Home—Lake Success, N. Y.
In 1955, Whitey pitched two consecu-
tive one-hitters, September 2 and 7. On
July 20, 1956, he tied the AL record by
fanning six men in a row at Kansas
City. His lifetime ERA is the lowest of
all Major League pitchers; his won-
lost percentage tops all active Major
League pitchers. Selected for All Star
Game 1954-55-56-59-60. Won two Se-
ries Games, 1960.

MAJOR LEAGUE PITCHING RECORD

	Games	IP	Won	Lost	Pct	Hits	Runs	ER	SO	Walks	ERA
1960	33	193	12	9	.571	168	76	66	85	65	3.08
LIFE	278	1,755	133	59	.693	1,469	607	527	1,000	729	2.70

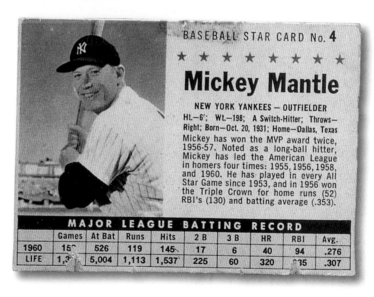

BASEBALL STAR CARD No. 4

★ ★ ★ ★ ★ ★ ★ ★ ★ ★

Mickey Mantle

NEW YORK YANKEES — OUTFIELDER

Ht.—6'; Wt.—198; A Switch-Hitter; Throws—
Right; Born—Oct. 20, 1931; Home—Dallas, Texas
Mickey has won the MVP award twice,
1956-57. Noted as a long-ball hitter,
Mickey has led the American League
in homers four times: 1955, 1956, 1958,
and 1960. He has played in every All
Star Game since 1953, and in 1956 won
the Triple Crown for home runs (52)
RBI's (130) and batting average (.353).

MAJOR LEAGUE BATTING RECORD

	Games	At Bat	Runs	Hits	2 B	3 B	HR	RBI	Avg.
1960	15?	526	119	145	17	6	40	94	.276
LIFE	1,3?	5,004	1,113	1,537	225	60	320	?15	.307

*A pretty nicely trimmed Mantle card from the 1969 Transogram box (top of page) leads off a group
of 1961 Post Cereal cards that didn't get the love usually afford to Yankee pasteboards.*

Rick Cerone souvenir button. (David Spindel Collection)

Roger Clemens

Steve Jacobson photo

Baseball Memorabilia
Print Series poster of Joe
DiMaggio by David Spindel,
original newspaper cartoon
autographed by DiMaggio
and a Greatest Sports
Legend video tape.
(David Spindel Collection,
www.spindelvisions.com)

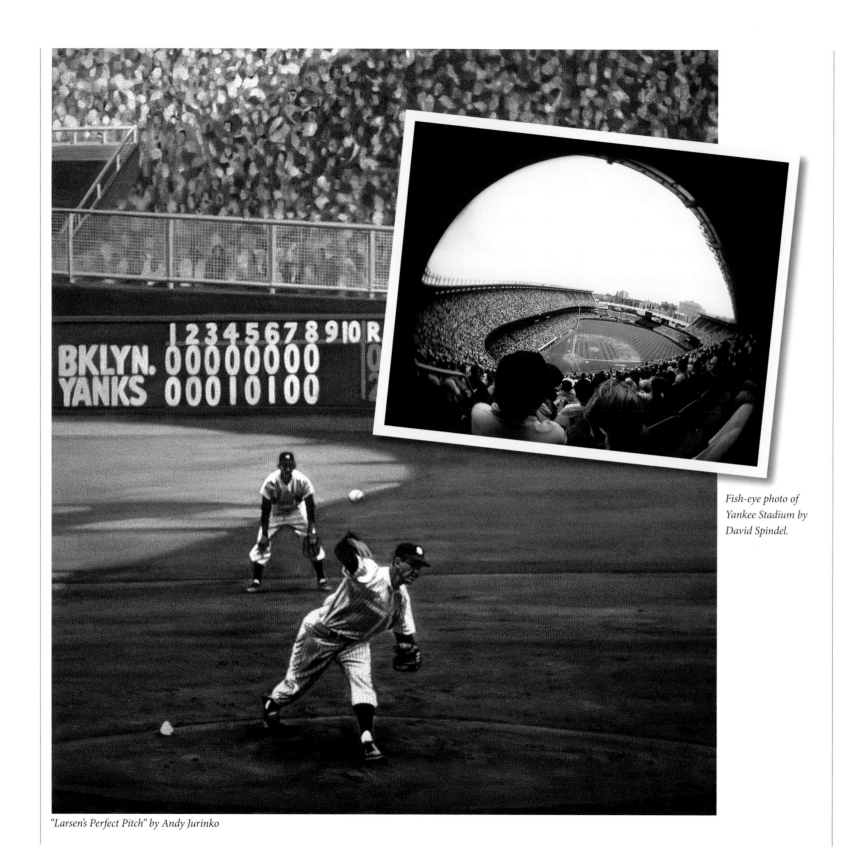

Fish-eye photo of
Yankee Stadium by
David Spindel.

"Larsen's Perfect Pitch" by Andy Jurinko

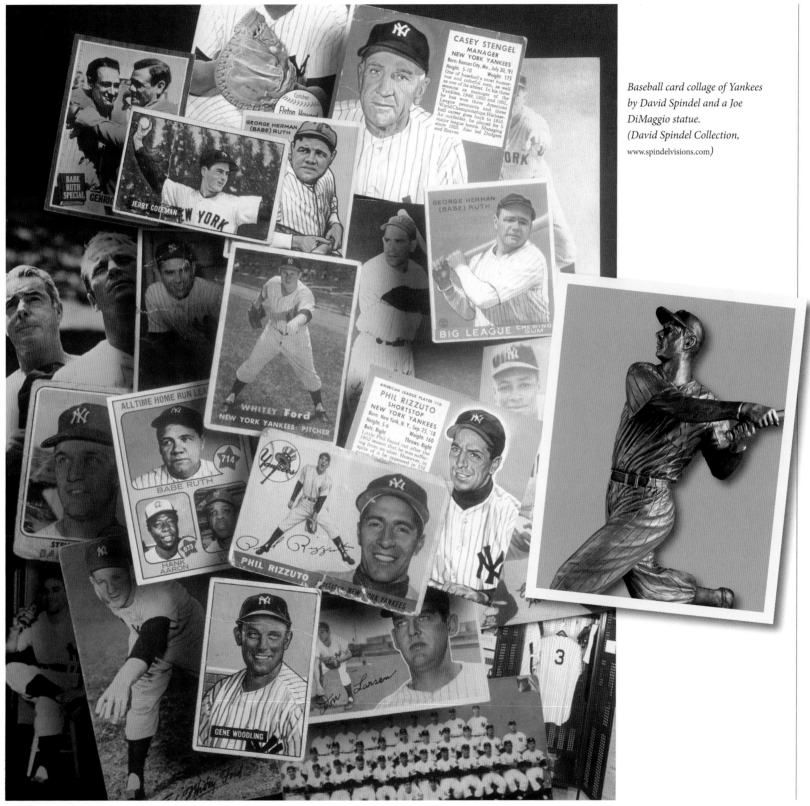

Baseball card collage of Yankees by David Spindel and a Joe DiMaggio statue.
(David Spindel Collection,
www.spindelvisions.com*)*

Yankee Stadium by Andy Jurinko.

Original pencil artwork by Ron Stark.

www.ronstarkstudios.com

To Barry
This is my 1956 Triple
crown. Glad to have
it as part of your
collection
Your Friend
Mickey Mantle

Seagram's

Triple Crown
1956
Mantle
P.C.T
.353

Mickey Mantle's Triple
Crown Award sold for
$211,500 in the 1999 Barry
Halper Auction in New York.

Sotheby's/Barry Halper

"Mantle's Perfect Catch"
by Andy Jurinko.

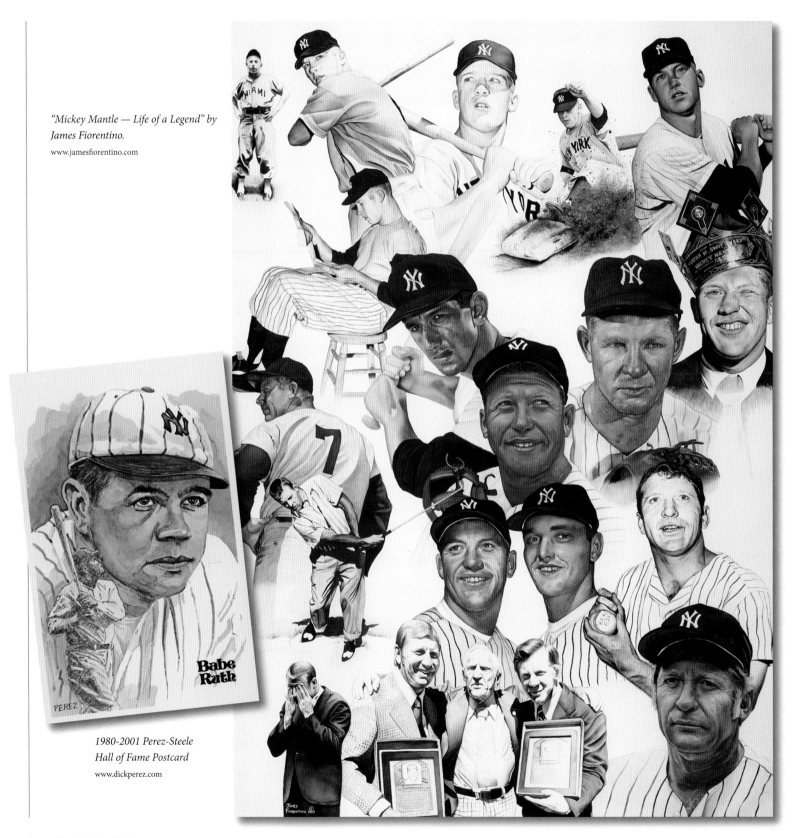

"Mickey Mantle — Life of a Legend" by James Fiorentino.

www.jamesfiorentino.com

*1980-2001 Perez-Steele
Hall of Fame Postcard*

www.dickperez.com

Mickey Mantle original artwork by Ron Stark.   www.ronstarkstudios.com

Chapter 7

The Mick

It was a story that Mickey Mantle used to relate to friends, a story he told and retold hundreds of times, always ending with the ballplayer in awe that his career playing a game, his life, could have meant so much to a fellow human being.

As he dutifully signs autographs one after another behind a long table in a hotel conference room or convention center, a middle-aged man slowly walks up to the table with a young son in tow. "There he is, son, that's The Mick," he will quietly tell the youngster.

And Mantle will see how moved the father is, sometimes the fan will be fighting back tears, and Mantle will shake his head as he retells the story, not comprehending how he could have had that kind of impact just from doing what came naturally to him.

It is said by Mantle's friends and close associates that by the time the Hall of Famer lay dying in a Texas hospital in 1995, he had a greater understanding of all that he had meant to a generation of baseball fans who grew up admiring him, and what he had meant to a couple of more generations after that who loved him nearly as much, often because their father told them that they must.

Mickey understood father and son stuff, too.

It's difficult for baby boomers to comprehend that for the several generations that have followed that 1946-64 frenzy of procreation, Mickey Mantle is as obscure and fuzzy an historical figure as Honus Wagner or Christy Mathewson. For the rest of us, it's a badge of considerable pride to be able to say, "I saw Mickey Mantle play at Yankee Stadium."

1959 Bazooka Gum

We wear it with some relish and a certain haughtiness.

To a greater degree than any athlete who has ever lived, Mantle is consecrated with a bevy of historical artifacts that keep him alive in a fashion never dreamed of by mortal men. And the most enduring of those artifacts are made of cardboard.

By the oddest of circumstances, not entirely fortuitous, his stamp was indelibly imprinted in that arcane world with the issuance of his 1952 Topps card late that summer. Widely but incor-

A nicely autographed Mickey Mantle cap.

Comedian Billy Crystal captivated the crowd on Day Five of the Halper Auction in 1999 when he ponied up $239,000 for Mickey's 1960 glove.   Sotheby's/Halper

rectly referred to as his "rookie" card (his actual rookie card is 1951 Bowman), the 1952 Topps card became for most Americans the most important and recognizable baseball card in the world.

That title may have been relinquished over the past decade or so as the Honus Wagner tobacco card sailed past the $1 million price tag and beyond, but that development hardly diminished the importance of that lustrous 1952 card.

What casual fans probably don't know is that part of the reason the card is so expensive stems from the fact that it was part of the last series from that famous 1952 issue (Topps' first full-size set), cards plunked down in the candy stores late in the summer. The cards did not sell as briskly as imagined, and in the years that followed Topps officials would try to peddle the returned inventory as prize premiums or fodder for vending machines at carnivals.

An estimated 400 cases or so languished in a Topps Brooklyn warehouse until around 1960 when Sy Berger, the executive most closely linked with four decades of Topps cards, had the pile loaded

Mickey's actual "rookie card," 1951 Bowman, is shown above; a Mint condition specimen sold for $135,343 in a 2007 Mastro Auction. At right is a 1962 Salada Coin.

onto a barge and quite unceremoniously dumped into the Atlantic Ocean.

That inglorious drowning helped make the Mantle card a lot tougher to find than the cards from the earlier series that year; Mickey did the rest in making the pasteboard so popular decades later. As the baseball card hobby was taking off in the early 1980s, three 1952 Mantles were sold at the famous Philly Card Show for about $3,000 each, grabbing national attention and helping to propel the notion of vintage baseball cards as investment devices as well as nostalgic treasures.

In 1986, the most famous baseball card dealer in America, Alan "Mr. Mint" Rosen, came upon a stash of uncirculated 1952 Topps cards in an elegant Quincy, Mass., home. Quite literally presented to him on a sterling-silver serving tray, the story goes that one of the many stacks of cards included 75 near-mint Mickey Mantles, half of them gem mint.

While the math can get fuzzy, it's certainly within reason to postulate that the Mantle "stack" alone from Rosen's historic find might be worth about $3.5 million dollars in 2009. Tallying up numbers for the Atlantic Ocean casualties gets a bit dicier; simply extrapolating numbers from what an unopened pack of high-number 1952

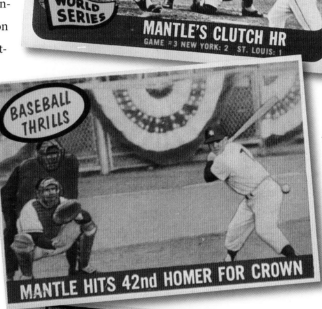

Topps might sell for yields a goofy number of $2 billion for those 400 cases.

And while his 1952 Topps card grabs the headlines (and sells for well above $100,000 in the highest grades), his 1951 Bowman rookie card can occasionally hit those kinds of numbers, too. A complete run of just one of each of Mantle's Topps and Bowman cards in the highest-grades attainable might cost the buyer $1 million or so.

Obviously, the prices become much more civilized when a collector is willing to tolerate card condition that doesn't simulate actual travel back in time.

But it's just that concept of time travel that helps keep alive the fervor for all things Mantle. Through an oddity involving the, uh, unconventional printing philosophies of the companies producing baseball cards in 2009 as opposed to 1952, Mantle, gone from this earthly plane for 13 years, has had literally thousands of "new" cards produced over that span. Considering only cards produced contemporaneously with his playing career, there might have been about 100, with perhaps a couple of dozen or so of those being the regular-issue cards that casual fans would recall decades later.

After Mantle's death in 1995, Topps had even gone the unusual route of

Three Mantle "Special" cards from 1965, 1959 and 1961 Topps sets.

The New York Daily News tells the story of a sad day for Yankee fans.

"retiring" a card number in their regular-issue sets; obviously, in this case Number 7. That curious homage was lifted several years later; by the time Topps reached an agreement with the Mantle estate for exclusive use of the Hall of Famer, that would shift from curious to ironic as the company would produce literally hundreds of "new" Mantle cards each year since 2006.

If any additional understanding of Mickey's unique hold on fans is needed, his link to yet another Yankee legend, Roger Maris, helps to explain it. Despite Mantle having essentially established his Hall-of-Fame credentials by the time Maris arrived via a Kansas City trade in 1960, he hadn't truly reached the revered status with Yankee fans that would be his ultimate legacy.

The laconic Maris, who quickly won two MVP Awards and helped send the club on another five-year streak of pennants, turned out to be a lightning rod for the nattering nabobs of the New York City press corps.

Where once they had been tough on Mantle, they now turned their occasional ire on the new costar. Seeing the taciturn Maris through the prism of the sportswriters, many Yankee fans were slow to warm up to him, even as he began his historic challenge of Babe Ruth's single-season home run record in 1961.

After what could only be described as an ordeal for the chain-smoking Maris, he found himself on Oct. 1, 1961, as the holder of a home run record that folklore suggests was stained by an asterisk. Stained, maybe, but not technically by that particular vexing notation.

In mid-season, as Mantle and Maris launched home runs at an unheard-of rate, Commissioner Ford Frick, once Babe Ruth's PR flak, intoned that unless the Ruth mark of 60 homers was bested in 154 or fewer games (the American League had expanded that year and upped the schedule to 162 games), they would be listed as separate records.

The acerbic Chipmunk sportswriter Dick Young is widely

Also shown (from top):
Mantle's 1953 Bowman
Color card; "Mickey
Mantle, 1956" by Andy
Jurinko (center) and
Mantle's autographed first
baseman's glove.
(glove from Hunt Auctions)

Mickey Mantle original artwork (left) by Arthur K. Miller.   www.artofthegame.com

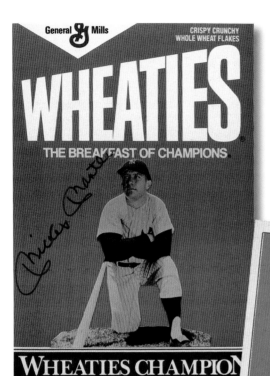

Even without any actual Wheaties, the promotional box (left) sold for $2,587 on the strength of Mickey's signature in the 1999 Barry Halper Collection Auction.
Sotheby's/Halper

Mantle cards from 1954 Red Heart Dog Food and 1958 (above) and 1962 Topps (right) are shown.

credited with promulgating the urban legend of the asterisk, which was never actually applied.

But much as it would be for Henry Aaron more than a decade later, the process of challenging a cherished record belonging to Ruth was a harrowing one. In Maris' case, it was made even more difficult because he had bested Mantle in the chase, with The Mick bowing out in the final weeks of the season with an injury.

"As far as I'm concerned, that's probably the greatest achievement in professional sports that I've ever seen," Mantle said in the interview in 1991. "Who was it that said there should be an asterisk? Ford Frick? They don't have it now and they never should have had it."

Mantle's defense of his friend (and part of the post-career golf crew) would remain a central theme in the decade that Mickey survived past Roger.

A movement still persists urging the election of Maris to the Hall of Fame, much as one continues in the same vein for Thurman Munson. While the technical arguments against their induction remain formidable, the sentiment of several generations of Yankee fans carries a weight not easily jostled by technical arguments.

❖

Mantle's foothold in the baseball card hobby made him a natural for the fledgling show-signing arena that blossomed in the 1980s and provided many multiples of career earnings for the elite autograph guests like Mantle, Joe DiMaggio and Ted Williams. Even for Mickey in the early 1980s, an autograph could be had at an East Coast card show for less than $10, but by the close of the decade it had zoomed to many times that number.

In the last years of his life, before being felled by the failed liver, he could make $50,000 or more for a weekend at a card show. And despite signing in staggering quantities perhaps only shy of the numbers put up in that department by Pete Rose, Mantle would take great care with his signature.

"If a kid is paying $30 for me to sign something for him, I feel

A Mickey Mantle memorabilia collage from Lelands.com Auctions, plus Mantle's 1980-2001 Perez-Steele Hall of Fame Art Postcard is at left.

Mantle's 1951 World Series bat (top, from Hunt Auctions),
plus three original paintings by Charles De Simone.

he's got a right to get a good signature. I see some kids come through the lines that don't look like they can afford it anyway ... I just feel I should do as good a job as I can."

Mantle's careful, concise autograph, naturally, became a favorite of the forger's arsenal, and tens of thousands of fake autographed items no doubt exist even to this day. When the FBI's Operation Bullpen in 2000 collared a forgery ring said to have produced $100 million in bogus memorabilia, Mantle items were among the most-forged names.

It is yet another tribute to his incredible stature that signed Mantle material seems to have emerged from that turning point largely unbowed. While such a debacle might have shattered the market for a lesser light's autograph entirely, the demand for Mantle-signed pieces continues unabated; a greater vigilance in terms of getting

third-party authentication has naturally also been a result of that historic sting.

The resilience of the Mantle name, coincidentally, was never more in evidence than three years after the Operation Bullpen takedown as the famed Guernsey's Auction house conducted a live auction at Madison Square Garden of material from the Mantle estate that totaled more than $4 million. Mickey's 1957 MVP Award fetched $321,000, his 1956 Silver Bat for winning the batting title brought $312,000, and his 1962 World Series ring went for $162,000. And proving that signatures with good provenance can still pack a lot of wallop, Mantle's individual player contracts from 1949-69 sold for a total of almost $700,000, which was not quite as much as the total dollar amount he was paid over that span.

Ironically, it was a Mickey Mantle bit of ephemera that would bear the signature of others, rather than the Mick, that would have a profoundly broader impact. In the years following his death, an organ donation card bearing Mickey's likeness and facsimile signature would encourage thousands of fans to fill out the cards and carry them in their wallets. That, were it his only legacy, would be enough to open the pearly gates for anyone.

Which, of course, was something Mantle had pondered and kiddingly concluded that he might have to grease St. Peter with a signed ball or two to ensure admittance.

❖

Often in America we wind up liking our heroes just a little bit flawed. The short answer is that it humanizes them, helps us keep them at least nominally down from that pedestal just a bit, which means we get a better, more up-close glimpse. Mickey Mantle was flawed just like that,

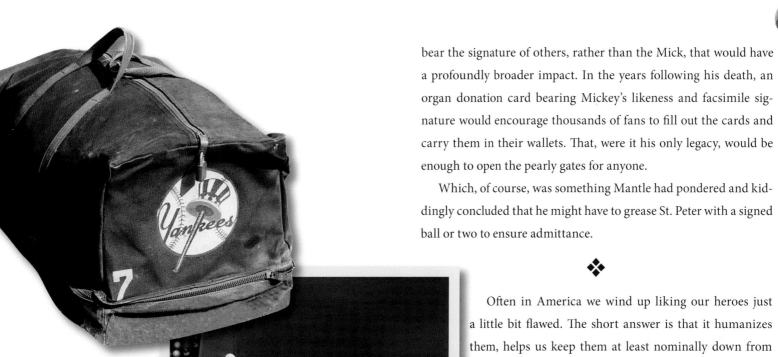

Mickey's No. 7 duffel bag and a Weekly Sports Illustrated magazine cover from 1956; at right, original Mantle artwork by Andy Jurinko.

only we didn't really know it until the end.

When he was playing, we thought it was the injuries that marred the otherwise perfect ballplayer. We wouldn't know really about the drinking and carousing until years later, learning first from a tell-all bestselling book and later from his fight for life at the end.

In a family ravaged by alcoholism, Mantle would ultimately come to terms with the disease and its impact on those around him, as well as on his own health. While there was some grumbling in the press about the circumstances surrounding his liver transplant two months before he died in August of 1995, it would have no real traction with an adoring public.

Bob Costas, a sportscaster and journalist of great renown, eulogized Mickey as "a fragile hero to whom we had an emotional attachment so strong and lasting that it defied logic." This from a man who idolized Mantle and even carried around a dog-eared 1958 Topps Mickey Mantle card in his wallet for much of his adult lifetime.

"In the last year of his life, Mickey Mantle, always so hard on himself, finally came to accept and appreciate the distinction between a role model and a hero," Costas continued. "The first, he often was not. The second, he always will be. And in the end, the people got it."

Mickey Mantle original artwork by Andy Jurinko (left) and Ron Stark (below).

MICKEY MANTLE
N. Y. YANKEES   OUTFIELD

"For people to still remember you and come up and have tears in their eyes and say that I was their boyhood idol and everything, it's pretty flattering."
– Mickey Mantle

"Portrait of Mantle" by Andy Jurinko.

Mickey Mantle original artwork by Andy Jurinko (left) and "Seven Up Still" (below) by Bill Williams.
www.goodsportsart.com

1980-2001 Perez-Steele Hall of Fame Postcards of Yogi Berra, Whitey Ford and Phil Rizzuto.

Perez-Steele Galleries
www.dickperez.com

Chapter 8

Berra, Ford and Rizzuto

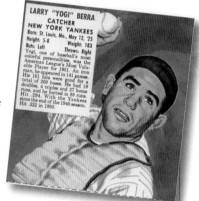

LARRY "YOGI" BERRA
CATCHER
NEW YORK YANKEES
Born: St. Louis, Mo., May 12, '25
Height: 5-8   Weight: 183
Bats: Left   Throws: Right
Yogi, one of baseball's most colorful personalities, was the American League's Most Valuable Player for 1951. An iron man, he appeared in 141 games. His 161 hits were good for a total of 269 bases. He had 19 doubles, 4 triples and 27 home runs, and he batted in 88 runs. Hit .294. With the Yankees since the end of the 1946 season. Hit .322 in 1950.

1952 Red Man Tobacco card

The greatest baseball player on the New York Yankees during their incredible run of 14 pennants in 16 seasons from 1949-64 was Mickey Mantle, but if the august body of sportswriters that covers Major League Baseball every year is to be duly acknowledged, the most-valuable player over that span may well have been Lawrence Peter Berra.

Indeed, the Baseball Writers' Association of America (BBWAA) concluded just that in 1951, 1954 and 1955, making "Yogi" Berra one of just eight players who have won the award three times. One other guy, Barry Bonds, won it seven times, but who's counting?

Imagine then that you are a player of such widely regarded talents, playing on perhaps the greatest dynasty in baseball history, and yet you wind up being remembered by future generations almost as much for your almost breathtaking malapropisms and a regrettable nickname linking you to a cartoon character as you are for your Hall-of-Fame statistics.

Berra's longevity through the Yankees' golden era brought him into the spotlight for some of the great moments in baseball history,

"It's always tough making predictions, especially about the future."

and not surprisingly, many of those took place in the World Series. So there was Berra, leaping into Don Larsen's arms following the final out of Game Six in the 1956 World Series, forever marking the moment of the only perfect game – or no-hitter, for that matter – in World Series history. And there was Berra, watching forlornly from left field as Bill Mazeroski's home run sailed over the wall at Forbes Field, ending that chaotic World Series in dark fashion for Yankees fans.

And none of that might have taken place at all if the machinations of another Hall of Famer, Branch Rickey, had panned out a little differently from Berra's days as a sandlot player in St. Louis. Berra and his pal, Joe Garagiola, another catcher, were spotted by the Cardinals' general manager.

In a tryout, Rickey told Berra, "Son, you'll never be a big-league ballplayer. You might be a Triple-A player." Yogi asked for the same

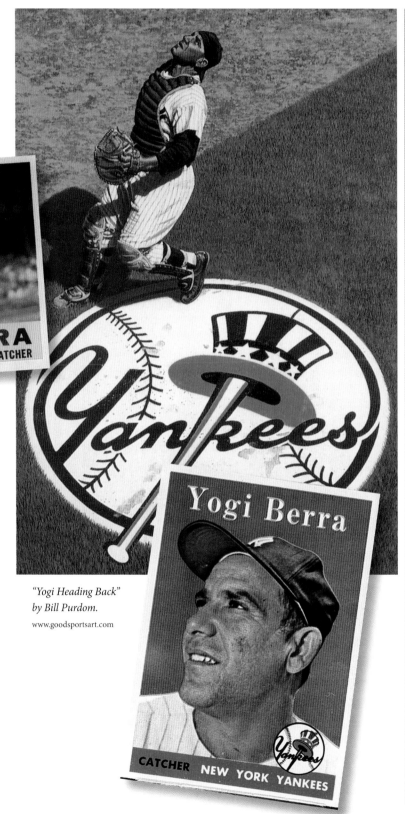

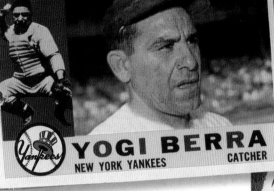

YOGI BERRA
NEW YORK YANKEES   CATCHER

$500 bonus that Garagiola got, but Rickey declined. Popular lore suggests that "The Mahatma," as Rickey was known, might have had more interest in "Yogi" than he was letting on. Rickey already had his sights set on a move to Brooklyn, and he may have been hoping to bring Berra to the Dodgers, but the Yankees intervened, $500 bonus in hand, and the rest is syntax-garbled history.

A notorious bad-ball hitter, he was as consistent a hitter as the American League had ever seen, socking 358 homers and driving in 1,430 runs in his 19-year career, yet he never led the American League in so much as one category over that span. Had there been an award for fewest strikeouts per at bat he might have snagged that easily; despite his penchant for swinging at anything he could reach with his lumber, his season-high strikeout total was 38. What Yogi would call a season's worth, Reggie Jackson might characterize as August.

That ability to hit just about anything and not strike out much in the process led to Berra's reputation as a "clutch hitter," the protestations of some of the modern statistical numbers crunchers

"Yogi Heading Back" by Bill Purdom.
www.goodsportsart.com

Yogi Berra

CATCHER   NEW YORK YANKEES

notwithstanding. There are SABRmaticians who insist that there is no such thing as a good "clutch hitter." I know a couple of generations of Bronx Bomber buffs who probably won't buy into this particular conclusion.

One of his great adversaries, Ted Williams, was disturbed by Berra's free-swinging philosophy, which was antithetical to Williams' own theories about only swinging at strikes and forsaking all others. Yogi even made matters worse by insisting on trying to engage the Splendid Splinter in informal chit-chat when he would come to the plate when Berra was handling the backstopping duties. "Doggone it, Yogi (or words to that effect), let me alone so that I can concentrate on my blankety-blank hitting," Ted was thought to have pleaded.

But Williams was one of the few asking for silence from Yogi, who was actually so nicknamed from what a childhood friend growing up in "The Hill" in St. Louis thought was a cosmic resemblance to a Hindu holy man. Berra would reportedly sit with his arms and legs crossed, seemingly in a meditative state, which prompted his pal, Bobby Hofman, to come up with the nickname.

For casual fans, it may come as something of a revelation that Berra didn't get the nickname from the Hanna-Barbera cartoon bear of similarly-sounding name. Instead, the anthropomorphic MVB of Jellystone Park was apparently named after the baseball player, though the animation studio denied that this was the case.

Even in these days of Orwellian spinning of otherwise incontrovertible evidence, that one seems like something of a reach. The bear turned up as part of the cast of "Huckleberry Hound," which debuted on television in 1958, by which time the other Yogi already had a fistful of World Series rings. The mannerisms of the bear were admittedly inspired by Ed Norton, one of the characters portrayed by the legendary television comedian Art Carney on "The Honeymooners."

It might even be a draw in trying to determine who was funnier, though Berra certainly gets the nod for apparently wading into the

1961 Post Cereal card and an autographed Gartlan statue.

Yogi's catcher's mitt. Hunt Auctions

Yogi Berra and Don Larsen original artwork by Andy Jurinko (below).

"Always go to other people's funerals, otherwise they won't come to yours."

profound, since even grammarians can't shake the suspicion that there may be something incredibly deep in pronouncements like, "It ain't over till it's over," or, "When you come to the fork in the road, take it."

While Berra is said to have been annoyed by the appropriation of his nickname by a cartoon character, the beloved "Yogi-isms" have long assumed a rightful place in Berra's colorful resume. It has also provided ammunition enough to make him a prolific author; his latest, "The Yogi Book," like many of the others, reached the *New York Times* Bestseller list.

History couldn't have come up with a more bizarre script for the 1949-64 Yankees if it had been crafted by Hollywood. A Hall-of-Fame catcher offering pearls like "Ninety percent of this game is half mental," laboring for a manager who makes Berra's linguistic gymnastics seem pedestrian by contrast.

"They say he's funny," Casey Stengel once offered in answering a question about his star catcher. "Well, he has a lovely wife and family, a beautiful home, money in the bank and he plays golf with millionaires. What's funny about that?"

And while Stengel, the master tactician posing as class clown, would have seemed a curious choice to lead the buttoned-down Yankees of the 1950s, who could have come up with the idea of Yogi as manager of the on-the-way-down edition of the team in 1964?

Just as the club itself seemed in disarray as that 1964 season unfolded, the choice of Berra as manager seems as incongruous now as it did at the time. Nobody questioned his knowledge of the game, but it was certainly a legitimate question to ask if he seemed like the ideal candidate to be enforcing discipline on a club saddled with aging stars and young wannabes who – as it turned out – would be heading into some of the storied franchise's darkest days.

Despite directing that graying aggregation into a final World Series in 1964, Berra was ousted after the World Series loss to St. Louis that fall. Later, he would sign on to coach for the (relatively) new kids in town: the New York Mets, who had also hired Casey

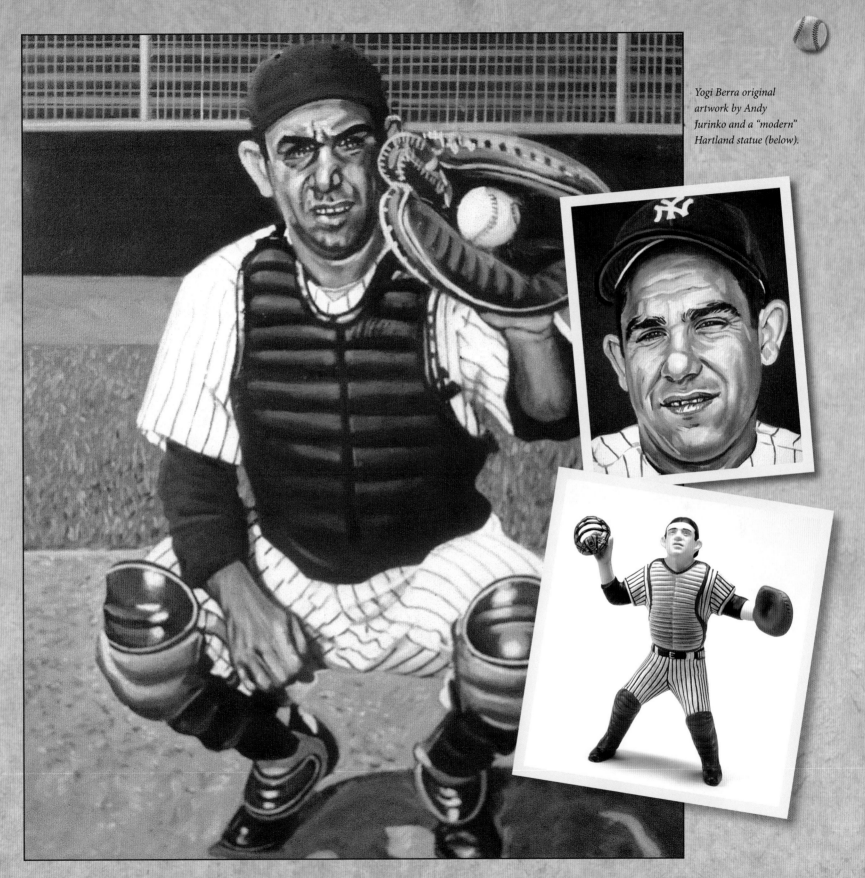

Yogi Berra original
artwork by Andy
Jurinko and a "modern"
Hartland statue (below).

Stengel as their first manager in 1962, launching a frenzy of hiring of former Yankees, Dodgers and Giants as a cheesy way of attracting fans in those early seasons.

It took fans quite a while to get used to seeing Berra in the orange and blue at Shea Stadium – and presumably some Bronx residents never quite managed it at all – but he did seem more suitably located as a base coach.

Yet there was more managing to come, as Berra would step in at the helm following Gil Hodge's death in 1972, and even led the Metsies to their second World Series in five years, though this time it wound up with an excruciating loss to the 1970s American League dynasty, the Oakland A's. That was the season that gave birth to the "It ain't over" observation, and indeed it wasn't, at least not until Charlie Finley's crew got ahold of them.

Yogi also got another crack at managing in 1984. After coming home to the Bronx as a coach amid much fanfare in 1976, he would be elevated to manager in 1984, managing just barely more than one full season in a period sandwiched by Billy Martin encores Nos. 3 and 4. Rudely fired by Steinbrenner after 16 games in 1985, a rift would develop between the Yankees' owner and the beloved Berra. It would last for 14 years, only to be lifted after a public apology to the Hall of Famer.

In the interim, Berra even had a three-year stint as a coach of the Houston Astros, and if you thought he looked out of place in a Mets uniform, you should see what the effect would be in the garish outfit from that era.

Ten years after his Houston venture, Berra wound up with perhaps the ultimate honor: his own museum. The Yogi Berra Museum and Learning Center opened on the campus of Montclair State University on September 21 as the Yankees played their final game at the Stadium, with no playoffs for the ball club in 2008.

Newspaper editors couldn't resist running Yogi's picture with the words, "It's over."

And it was.

❖

Whitey Ford

It is a testimony to the unique status the Yankees had achieved from the end of World War II to the mid-1960s expansion of the Vietnam War that team members would anguish over their rare World Series losses far more than they did over their much more frequent victories.

Thus did Whitey Ford, "The Chairman of the Board," of a ball club noted for its corporate boardroom-like efficiency on the field, fret for decades about the Yankees' heart-stopping defeat in the 1960 World Series at the hands of Bill Mazeroski and his ninth-inning Forbes Field home run.

The Yankees' ace had been the Game One pitcher in Fall Classics from 1955-58, but Casey had a bit of inspiration and decided to send Art Ditmar out to begin the Forbes Field festivities. He didn't make it through the first inning, and the Yankees eventually lost, 6-4.

Ford would not pitch until the teams returned to Yankee Stadium knotted at 1-1. He pitched a pair of shutouts in a Series where the Bronx Bombers outscored the Forbes Field gang 55-27, recording wins of 16-3, 12-0 and 10-0, those last two part of Ford's historic World Series record of 33-2/3 scoreless innings. That one stood virtually unchallenged in the record books until a later generation Yankee, reliever Mariano Rivera, pushed it aside in 2000. Of course, Rivera's 34-2/3 innings is a postseason record; if you only count the World Series, Ford is likely to reign in that particular category for a long, long time.

"If the World Series was on the line and I could pick one pitcher to pitch the game, I'd choose Whitey Ford every time." No less an authority than Mickey Mantle came up with that one. In hindsight, Casey's decision to hold Ford until Game Three in that World Series – and potentially even more broadly Stengel's usage of the left-hander through most of Ford's career – may have been faulty.

For the eight years when Stengel would have Ford's services available on a full-time basis, he was usually limited to about 30 starts per year, a rate of activity that effectively put the 20-win plateau out of reach. Yankee fans from the era will recall that much of that careful spotting of Ford starts was aimed at saving his ace for particular rivals or contenders as Stengel built his reputation as a master strategist.

Once Ralph Houk took the helm following Stengel's post-Mazeroski firing, Ford got 38-39 starts for the next three years, and recorded his two career-high win totals of 25 and 24. I'll leave it to Stengel supporters to argue that suddenly upping Ford's annual workload by 40-50 innings was a good idea for a 35-year-old hurler who had been so carefully used up to that point.

Ford and Stengel had another point of intersection: even at the time of the dynasty and certainly in the four decades since it ended, both have had to contend with the widely held belief that their success was largely the result of having been a part of such great teams.

For Stengel, it manifested itself in the "push-button manager" allegation; for Ford, it was an assertion that reached the level of conventional wisdom that those flashy won-loss totals (25-4, 24-7, 19-6, for example) wouldn't have been possible with lesser clubs.

Like most such pearls, there may be just enough truth in them to provide some validity, but in Ford's case it's worth noting that his 2.75 lifetime ERA also was markedly better than any of his contemporaries, and that his winning percentage was significantly higher than what the club managed in those games where he did not appear.

Whitey's 1953 Bowman Color is shown on the facing page; original Ford artwork by Andy Jurinko is at the top of the page, along with his 1966 Topps card (above) and a signed Gartlan Statue.

When he hung it up as injuries took their toll in the mid-1960s, Ford's 236-106 record left him with the highest winning percentage in history at .690.

In the end, though, Whitey Ford was hardly defined by numbers, however spectacular. He was part of one of the great buddy stories in baseball lore, storming around The Big Apple and American League cities with Mickey Mantle and creating a friendship that would last nearly a half-century.

They were barely old enough to vote when they were thrust in the middle of an already impressive Yankee dynasty. Ford started out in 1950 with about as big a bang as any pitcher ever: he won his first nine decisions before losing a game in relief. Once Ford had completed his Army service in 1952-53, he returned to a Yankee team where Mantle was now the established star and the club was warming up for a four-pennant run from 1955-58.

Various reference works attribute Whitey's other nickname, "Slick," to cliched notions about his being a crafty left-hander, as he was so often described. He may indeed have been crafty, with the odd moistened or disfigured baseball here and there, but that wasn't the source of the name.

"I never threw the spitter, well maybe once or twice when I really needed to get a guy out real bad," Ford said, but added that the "Slick" appellation came from elsewhere. "Casey called the three of us 'Whiskey Slick,' "

Whitey Ford artwork by Andy Jurinko.

Ford continued. It was a reference to the Three Amigos: Mantle, Ford and Billy Martin. "Mickey then cut it short to 'Slick.' It was always his name for me, and he liked it."

To say that the Yankees were on top of the world in those days is understatement without equal. Long before professional sports stars had reached the tax brackets and trappings of the icons of Hollywood and rock and roll, the Yankees of the 1950s-60s understood what it all meant.

Ford likes to reminisce about a spring training trip in 1961 or 1962 when the team traveled to Palm Beach from Fort Lauderdale for a ball game, making the trip by bus in their uniforms.

"I went into the dressing room for a smoke," Ford said almost apologetically in relating the story long after he had pushed aside the evil habit. "And two guys in suits walked in and flashed a badge and said, 'Who are you?' and I said, 'Whitey Ford.' And they said, 'Good, just who we are looking for.' "

They explained they were Secret Service and they were there at the behest of Joe Kennedy, the President's father, who was inviting some of the players to his Palm Beach home. And off they went to the Kennedy compound, riding in the limousine in their baseball duds.

Displaying spectacular hobby sensibilities so many years before there was really a hobby, Ford took along a dozen baseballs, and then mustered up the chutzpah to ask the 73-year-old patriarch of the Kennedy clan if he would be willing to get his famous son to sign and inscribe the balls to the players.

"And I reminded him that they should be inscribed, 'To Tony (Kubek), To Mickey, To Whitey, etc.' And sure enough, about a month later I got them back in the mail. There were three of each, and I gave them to the guys."

There's a kind of cosmic, ironic justice in pro ballplayers managing to make a couple of bucks off someone famous signing a baseball for them.

Signing autographs, which Ford and Mantle had done so much as a matter of course during their playing careers, would be thrust back into their lives as a second career in the late 1970s as the baseball card hobby boomed. And it would be a second link between the two great friends, one that would flourish for nearly 20 years until his friend died so young and so dramatically in the national spotlight.

Whitey, the ultimate sidekick, has dutifully carried on the legacy of his lifelong pal.

Whitey Ford original artwork by Andy Jurinko (right); below is a Ford jersey and Hall of Fame Commemorative Plate from the David Spindel Collection.
www.spindelvisions.com

Whitey Ford photo by Steve Jacobson.

❖ Phil Rizzuto

Joe DiMaggio had his inclusion in "The Old Man and the Sea," Yogi Berra had an obnoxious cartoon bruin named after him and Babe Ruth was so famous that Japanese soldiers tried to antagonize GI's by shouting disparaging epithets about him, but for cultural linkages for a sports star, Phil Rizzuto's inclusion in Meatloaf's 1977 rock anthem "Paradise by the Dashboard Light" may just be the best ever.

It's also appropriate that perhaps the most beloved member of the Yankee family would have such an unprecedented role in a bawdy bit of rock and roll, Phil's public denials aside about not understanding the rollicking bit of double entendre embedded in his play-by-play of a player rounding the bases. Ahem.

For the man who bridged several generations of Yankee fans and was on hand as a player or broadcaster for championships spanning six decades, the resurgence of notoriety beyond the friendly confines of Metropolitan New York was timely indeed. It came around the time that a groundswell of support for his Hall-of-Fame candidacy was starting to take root; by the time the song had achieved

1956 Topps

"classic" status just like Rizzuto, the shortstop was finally honored with a plaque in Cooperstown.

For his legion of fans, the vast majority of which knew him only from dusty old record books or, more likely, from his alternately homespun and hilarious work in the broadcast booth, this was only justice long overdue. Scooter and Pee Wee (Reese) had been the top shortstops in Major League Baseball in the 1940s and 1950s, and his Dodger rival would reside with the other immortals for a full decade before the 1950 MVP would join him in 1994.

It was a sore point for his fans at the time, and hardly has been completely disposed of in the years following his induction. The charming debate that gives so much vibrancy to Hall of Fame watchers continues even to this day, with detractors – and numbers crunchers – insisting that Rizzuto simply doesn't have the stats to warrant his inclusion.

What they run afoul of is the inherent bias shown to home run hitters and flashy batting averages, and a corresponding discounting of all things defensive. But nobody discounted anything when he was playing and helping lead the Yankees to 10 pennants in his 13 seasons. He was a spark plug on offense and a magician on defense. By teammates and foes alike, the 5-6, 150-pound Rizzuto was regarded as a fierce competitor, no small praise indeed for a player surrounded by a squadron of talented superstars of every description.

The 1950 American League MVP retired with a boatload of career and single-season fielding records, despite playing "only" 11 full seasons and parts of two others at the end. Like so many of his contemporaries, he also missed three full seasons in his prime, serving in the Navy during World War II.

Not surprisingly, he also holds more than a half-dozen World Series fielding records and ranks in the top 10 of a number of offensive categories as well.

He impressed no less of a crusty dinosaur than Ty Cobb, who called Rizzuto "one of two modern ballplayers who could have held their own among old-timers." Stan Musial was the other.

In a celebrated encounter long before Stengel would be named to manage the Yankees in 1949, he had thoroughly dissed Rizzuto during a Brooklyn Dodgers tryout by advising him "to go get a shoebox." This may have been a point of some additional bonding between Scooter and Yogi, who had been similarly rejected by a notable Brooklyn executive early in his career.

And the devotion of Yankee fans and the near-unanimous regard of his contemporaries notwithstanding, Rizzuto's unseemly dismissal by Yankees executives late in 1956 illustrated the uncomfortable duality that always existed in the game. It was a game, for sure, but it was also a business, and reconciling the two was no simpler in that era than it is today.

Called in to a meeting ostensibly to go over the roster with front office staffers, Rizzuto was asked to look for names of players who might be cut to make room for post-season addition Enos Slaughter. After some back and forth and reasons offered why each of his

Phil Rizzuto original artwork (above) and "Scooter Turning Two" by Andy Jurinko.
www.goodsportsart.com

Phil Rizzuto Baseball Hero magazine at left. (David Spindel Collection)

suggestions probably wouldn't work, Rizzuto realized that he was the expendable Yankee.

Rizzuto, understandably stung by the hamhanded maneuver, resisted the urge to denounce the malefactors after listening to sage advice from a former teammate, George "Snuffy" Stirnweiss, who counseled him not to burn any bridges. That's worthwhile guidance for anybody in similar circumstances; in Scooter's case it helped pave the way for a 40-year broadcasting stint.

There are a lot of Italian restaurants in New Jersey that benefitted from that advice almost as much as Rizzuto did.

(David Spindel Collection)

*Phil Rizzuto original
artwork by Andy Jurinko
and Rizzuto's 1951 Topps
Major League All Stars card.*

Andy Jurinko artwork of (from top, L-R): Allie Reynolds, Hank Bauer, Tommy Henrich, Charlie Keller, Billy Johnson, Joe Page, Bob Grim and Gene Woodling.

Chapter 9

The Supporting Cast

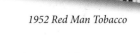

GIL MC DOUGALD
SECOND BASE
NEW YORK YANKEES
Born: San Francisco, Cal., 5-19-'28
Height: 6-1   Weight: 180
Bats: Right   Throws: Right
The American League's Rookie of the Year, Gil did a sensational job for the 1951 World Champions, playing at both second and third. He was in 131 games, had 123 hits, including 23 doubles, 4 triples and 14 home runs, and he batted in 63 runs. His average was .306, the only Yankee regular to hit over .300. Batted in 6 runs in one inning to tie a major league record.

1952 Red Man Tobacco

Baseball is the grandest of all professional sports for a number of reasons, but one of the most compelling is the realization that no other sport so uniquely blends the heroics of the individual with the communal joys and rewards of teamwork. A player can win the game seemingly single-handedly with a walk-off home run in extra innings, but it no doubt took the labors of many others to make that giddy event possible in the first place.

Baseball also rewards its individuals with the grandest of all nods to immortality: the Baseball Hall of Fame, founded in 1936, has been the prototype for similar undertakings in sports both professional and amateur, and also in virtually every walk of life from the Chamber of Commerce to the Benevolent and Protective Order of Eagles.

And so the New York Yankees have parlayed 85 years of extraordinary success at their beloved Stadium with a roster of legendary individuals into more Hall of Fame plaques in Cooperstown than imaginable. Yet despite all of that, the 26 world championships from that tenure are the handiwork of a marvelous supporting cast as much as they are from the Cooperstown ghosts.

Indeed, many of those we've lumped into the "Supporting Cast" chapter have their own plaques in the bucolic hamlet in Central New York. They managed to grab the immortality golden ticket despite being overshadowed by many of the brightest lights on the stage.

Tony Lazzeri, Earle Combs and Bob Meusel were vital components in the famous "Murderer's Row" Yankees squads of the 1920s, yet while "Poosh 'Em Up" Tony and Combs were inducted, Meusel, he of cantankerous personality and often questionable work ethic, was not.

The Yankees in those days were thought to have been such an offensive juggernaut that pitching was an afterthought, but true students of the game realize that rarely does a team get to the World Series with less-than-stellar pitching.

When the Yankees nailed down that first World Series win in

★ ★ ★ **No. 16** ★ ★ ★

Roger Maris

NEW YORK YANKEES — OUTFIELDER

Ht. 6'0"; Wt. 204; Bats Left; Throws Right;
Born September 10, 1934; Home: Raytown, Mo.
Fans will long remember Roger's feat of 61
HRs in the 1961 season, establishing a record
for a 162-game schedule. Named Player of the
Year by the Sporting News for 1961 and AL
MVP in 1960-61, he led the AL in RBIs (112)
in 1960, in 1961 with 142, and received the
Gold Glove Award as AL outstanding right
fielder in 1960. Roger hit a HR the first time
at bat in the 1960 World Series. He has played
in 7 All-Star Games.

★ ★ **MAJOR LEAGUE BATTING RECORD** ★ ★ ★

	Games	At Bat	Runs	Hits	2B	3B	HR	RBI	Avg.
1962	157	590	92	151	34	1	33	100	.256
LIFE	842	3053	539	793	117	28	191	557	.260

*"Celebrating Cone's
Perfection" by Bill
Purdom.*
www.goodsportsart.com

*August 1961 Life
magazine.*

1923 in spanking their landlord, John McGraw in six games, they did it with pitching as much as from thumping, though someone named Ruth did have three home runs and scored eight times.

"Bullet Joe" Bush, Bob Shawkey, Sam Jones, Waite Hoyt, and Herb Pennock anchored that staff that led the league in ERA while Ruth clubbed more homers during the season than several teams. Hoyt and Pennock would be joined by Urban Shocker a couple of years later, and all three would eventually be reunited in Cooperstown, but still-misty history remembers those glorious Yankee teams of the 1920s for the sluggers, not the moundsmen. One suspects it's a level of anonymity those players were happy to accept right along-side the World Series checks, which for many players in those days might represent a good chunk of their annual income.

By 1930, a Hall of Fame catcher had joined the lineup, Bill Dickey, and Shawkey returned now as manager, taking over from Artie Fletcher, who had finished out the 1929 campaign after Huggin's death in late September. The pitching was still solid and the offense

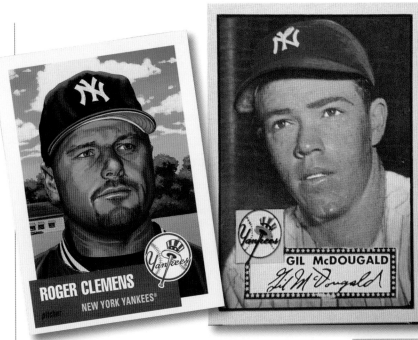

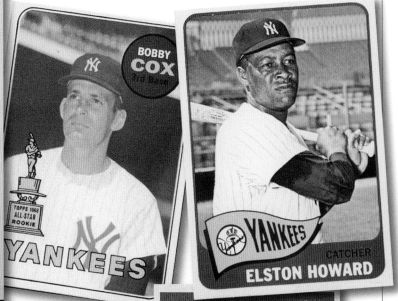

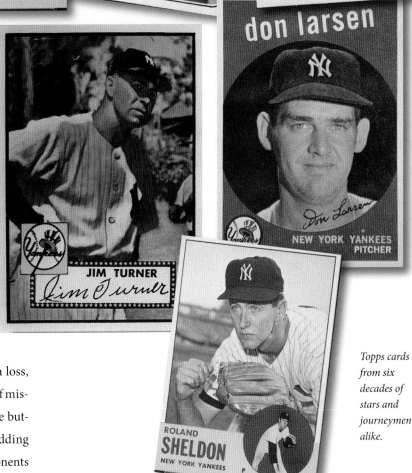

obviously still formidable with Ruth and Gehrig hitting 90 round trippers between them, but by then Connie Mack's A's were the Toast of the American League.

By the time the Yankees got back to the World Series in 1932 to sweep the Cubs – including Ruth's alleged called shot – the pitching staff had added a couple more Hall of Famers, Lefty Gomez and Red Ruffing. The prankster Gomez was notorious for his high jinks, including taking a ground ball off the mound and flinging it to a bewildered Lazzeri instead of starting a double play by throwing it to shortstop Frank Crosetti. "I couldn't think of which Italian to throw to," is how history records his explanation to a livid but nearly speechless Joe McCarthy.

But Gomez would win 20 games for the Yankees four times in the 1930s, and notch six World Series wins without a loss, the kind of stats that would allow any ball club to tolerate a bit of mischief. Despite the Yankees' eventual reputation as the ultimate button-down franchise, it was also to be one that didn't blink at adding some eccentric to the roster if he carried the other vital components of "The Yankee Mystique." A manager in 1949 who could garble the

Topps cards from six decades of stars and journeymen alike.

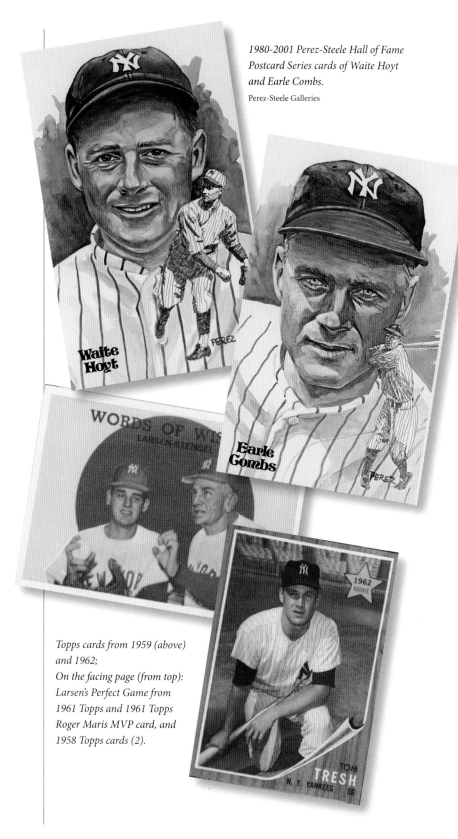

1980-2001 Perez-Steele Hall of Fame Postcard Series cards of Waite Hoyt and Earle Combs.

Perez-Steele Galleries

Topps cards from 1959 (above) and 1962;
On the facing page (from top): Larsen's Perfect Game from 1961 Topps and 1961 Topps Roger Maris MVP card, and 1958 Topps cards (2).

English language like no other, a hard-throwing right-hander and later best-selling author, a harmonica-playing utility infielder and an absolutely unique flake who was perfect for the 1970s all owe their spot in Yankees lore to that laudable philosophy.

Of the aforementioned Casey Stengel, Jim Bouton, Phil Linz and Mickey Rivers, each played a vital role on different squads, with Casey obviously marshalling all his curious strategies and eccentricities to orchestrate the amazing seven World Series titles and 10 pennants in 12 seasons.

But Stengel was toiling in nearby Brooklyn for the Dodgers in the mid-1930s when Joe DiMaggio showed up and put in motion the forces that would propel the club to its most glorious stretch up to that time. "Old Reliable" Tommy Henrich joined the club in 1937, and Charlie Keller two years later, forming a Bronx Bomber outfield trio that would neatly flank DiMaggio (along with Twinkletoes Selkirk until World War II broke out) for most of the decade of the 1940s.

And while Henrich earned the "Old Reliable" monicker, it could just as easily have been applied to second baseman (and later a long-time AL manager) Joe Gordon, who was called "The greatest all-around ballplayer I ever saw, and I don't bar any of them," by his manager, Joe McCarthy. His timely hitting and acrobatic fielding skills combined to win Gordon the 1942 MVP Award (and a 2009 Hall of Fame nod), besting Triple-Crown winner Ted Williams, who would ultimately become accustomed to being denied such laurels largely based on the fact that he was not surrounded by quite as much talent as were his contemporaries down Interstate 95.

Through the war years the Yankees pitching staff was as unsettled as the rest of the league's, but by the time the boys came marching home, they were on the verge of adding the names that would pitch them through the first half of that great 1949-60 dynasty: Allie Reynolds (1947), Eddie Lopat and Vic Raschi (both in 1948).

That triumvirate would win 53 games between them in 1949 (reliever Joe Page chipped in a league-leading 27 saves) as the club won World Series No. 1 of a staggering five in a row. And they did it with an outfield of .... drum roll, please .... Hank Bauer, Cliff Mapes and Gene Woodling.

OK, they also had an injured guy named DiMaggio turning in a brilliant half-season despite the ravages of the march of time, but the season put Stengel's soon-to-be-revered platooning skills on display for the first time.

Three more big years from Reynolds, Lopat and Raschi, plus 15 wins from fireballing Tommy Byrne and it all added up to a World Series sweep of an aggregation called "The Whiz Kids," who apparently didn't whiz much in October.

DiMaggio bowed out after the 1951 campaign, but there seemed to be a suitable replacement on hand: a young phenom from Oklahoma named Mickey Mantle. Stengel was still making ballplayers mad and Yankee front-office types deliriously happy as he platooned to winning effect, utilizing an aging slugger acquired from the crosstown rival Giants, Johnny Mize, and a brilliant young ballplayer, Gil McDougald, who seemed willing – and able – to perform ably at whatever skill position Casey planted him in the infield.

But McDougald's relationship with the eccentric manager was rocky, with the youngster chafing more than a little from Casey's prodding. The infielder finally confronted him: "Why don't you get rid of me? You're going to give me an ulcer."

"Gil, you're a better ballplayer when you're mad," Stengel replied. "I figured I'd keep you mad."

"That's all right from your standpoint, but not from mine," McDougald told him. And the skipper eased up a bit and found other ways to try to motivate him, at least for the second half of McDougald's sterling 10-year career.

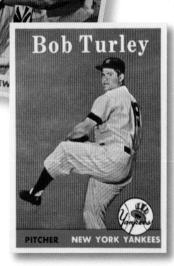

Mize would, like so many other Yankees, wind up with a bronze plaque in Cooperstown, but that honor didn't stem from his heroics at Yankee Stadium. A four-time NL homer champ, he would provide only about four dozen in barely more than four seasons, but it's probably worth noting that "The Big Cat" also cashed a World Series check all four years.

The penchant for platooning that helped solidify Stengel's genius status wasn't always enthusiastically embraced by the platoonees. The World War II decorated Marine Hank Bauer remembered socking two home runs and a double against Detroit, only to have Stengel send in Woodling late in the game to pinch hit for him.

"The score was tied, 5-5, in the eighth inning, and I was up there hitting when they brought in a right-hander. I almost sawed Gene's legs off. He didn't want to come up. When I walked into the dugout, Casey said to me, 'I thought you had your quota.' "

But ultimately, Bauer and others saw it in another light. "I played until I was 39. One day I got together with Woodling and said, 'You know, we complained about platooning with Stengel, but we we're around a long time.' Woodling played until he was 40. I didn't like being platooned but we won every year, so what can you say?"

But it wasn't all musical chairs. Over the years until it all fell apart in 1965, the team would boast All-Stars like Bobby Richardson, Tony Kubek, Elston Howard, Bill Skowron, Clete Boyer, Joe Pepitone, and Tommy Tresh, plus world-beater hurlers who might have gained more individual notoriety as bigger fish in smaller ponds, but liked the World Series checks, too.

Playing in an era when the World Series booty could amount to a large fraction of annual pay, pitchers like Bullet Bob Turley, Johnny Kucks, Tom Sturdivant, Duke Maas, Art Ditmar, Ralph Terry, Bill Stafford, Jim Bouton, and Al Downing all found it quite comforting to play second fiddle to Whitey Ford.

Roger Maris was nobody's second fiddle; in fact, upon arrival in New York in 1960 he quickly won MVP Awards his first two seasons, highlighted by the epic 1961 home run chase with teammate Mickey Mantle.

But his 61-home run season that year was as bittersweet as Henry Aaron's historic breaking of the all-time home run record 13 years later. Tackling the ghost of Babe Ruth turned out to be even more trying than trying to sneak a fastball past the live one.

For Maris there was the added aggravation of his seemingly upstaging The Mick, whose popularity actually jumped quite a bit those first years with Roger preceding him in the batting order. The rancor of the New York media frequently shifted to Maris, who despite being a wonderful all-around ballplayer, was never able to live up to the unrealistic expectations that followed that giddy season.

As the Yankees horrified their followers by plunging to the bottom of the American League in 1966, Mantle was ailing mightily and clearly on the decline, Ford was all but finished and Maris was shipped off to St. Louis, were the fates conspired to give him a much-deserved break. Released from his purgatory where he would never have been able to match what he had once been able to do, he was heartily embraced in St. Louis for what he had always been: a fine, hustling ballplayer, with marvelous baseball instincts and a bit of pop still left in his bat. It didn't hurt that St. Louis found itself in the World Series in both of Maris' final two campaigns.

Topps cards from 1954 (right), 1957 (above left) and 1956 are shown.

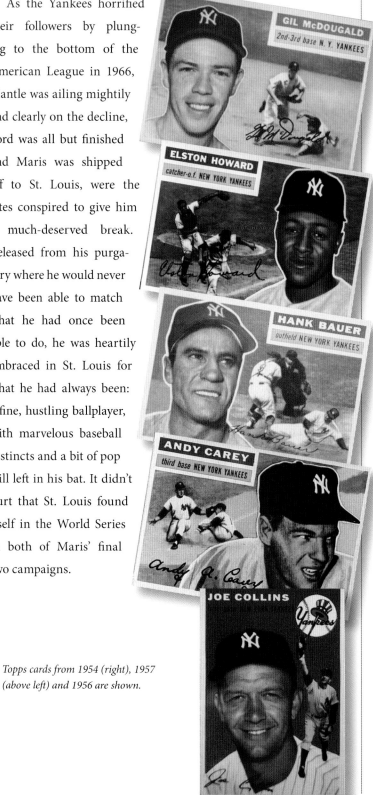

With Mantle's retirement after the icky 1968 season, the Yankees would metaphorically wander in the desert for years to come. The next year the leagues expanded to 12 teams each, and promptly divvied things up in East/West divisions. The World Series, once seemingly the Yankees' birthright every October by way of regular-season prowess, would now have to be attained through an additional layer of competition: the playoffs.

It only seemed fitting that now with the top prize no longer anointed in the same fashion, the bully boys from the Bronx who had cornered it for so many years would no longer be much of a factor.

There were rock-solid pitchers: Mel Stottlemyre, Fritz Peterson and Stan Bahnsen were hardly chopped liver, but some of the everyday names got curiouser and curiouser, at least by Yankee standards. Danny Cater, Horace Clarke, Gene Michael, Jerry Kenney and Curt Blefary – decent ballplayers all, but not able to dislodge the storied franchise from this new and uncomfortable mediocrity.

But help was on the way, and in some instances already there. A brash young catcher named Thurman Munson seemed to radiate the kind of qualities that had been a hallmark of so many giants of earlier decades. A quiet, talented outfielder named Roy White had actually been with the team since 1965 and would not get to a World Series game until his 12th Yankee season, but would retire with a place firmly planted on the team's all-time rankings in a host of offensive categories.

A teammate of White's from that inglorious 1965 debacle, Bobby Murcer, would end up no less revered by serious Yankee fans, but the fates would be even rougher with him: he was the team's marquee player for the whole dry spell, then was shipped off to the San Francisco Giants in 1975 just as his former team was starting to show signs of life.

Early in the 1974 season, a big first baseman named Chris Chambliss arrived from the Cleveland Indians, the same team

Bill Skowron's 1954 Topps rookie card leads off; Allie Reynolds' 1954 Bowman bats seventh – the rest are 1953 Topps.

1953 Bowman Allie Reynolds (left) and 1954 Bowman Vic Raschi.

The new "TV" craze is celebrated with 1955 Bowmans.

that had coughed up a third baseman a year earlier: Graig Nettles. The former was a gifted first sacker, with good power and an even better work ethic; the latter had even more power and a Gold Glove at third. This seemed promising. All-Stars at catcher, center field and the corners of the infield. You didn't have to be Branch Rickey to see that the elements of a winning team were falling into place.

With such a nucleus the team barely missed winning the AL East that year, coming up short by only two games behind the East's powerhouse, the Baltimore Orioles. Pat Dobson and Doc Medich headed a decent pitching staff that was about to become so much better. In a carnival sideshow of staggering debauchery, major league owners would wrestle over who could sign the game's first real free agent, Catfish Hunter, after Oakland A's owner Charlie Finley foolishly allowed his star pitcher to get away.

Hunter had been a 20-game winner for four straight years as the A's had nailed down three World Series titles in a row, but now he was a Yankee, pitching on the grandest stage in the world and doing it for a bigger pile of dough than anybody could ever imagine. Turns out, we just hadn't been letting our imaginations have free enough rein.

With his cash safely tucked away, Hunter won 23 games for George Steinbrenner and Co. in 1975, and the team finished third. The next year Hunter added 17 more, the team added a second baseman named Willie Randolph and the club won the AL East and a thrilling five-game American League Championship Series against the Kansas City Royals. That last item came by way of a walk-off home run by Chambliss.

As would be the case in many a major league season over coming decades, the World Series would find the playoffs to be a tough act to follow. After waiting 14 years to see their favorites back performing on their favorite stage, Yankee fans had to endure a quick four-game drubbing by the vaunted Cincinnati Reds.

But more elements were being added all the time. Mickey Rivers, he of enormous speed, considerable batting skills, a throwing arm like Betty Crocker and the perpetrator of linguistic absurdities and malaprops that would make Norm Crosby (or maybe Yogi Berra) proud, arrived in 1976 from the California Angels. The center fielder's impact was immediate: 43 stolen bases and 95 runs scored thrilled Yankees fans, while his colorful quotes entertained a Big Apple media throng that could finally be able to scribble down something other than traditional hackneyed baseball-speak.

One of Rivers' gems was directed at the guy who would turn up in 1977. "No wonder you're all mixed up. You got a white man's first name, a Spanish man's second name and a black man's third name," Rivers told Reginald Martinez Jackson.

The exchanges between the two would become classics, but all the hoopla aside, Jackson's principal contribution was with his bat, though his lips came in a solid second.

The pennant-winning Yankee teams in the 1970s were solid virtually from top to bottom in the field, but they also had pitching as good as any in the league, which was saying something in a division with the pitching-rich Orioles and Luis Tiant at the top of his game in Boston.

By 1976, as America went bonkers over the Bicentennial, Ed Figueroa and Doc Ellis proved to be a nice complement to ace Hunter; they also had a flaky relief pitcher named Sparky Lyle, who would nicely handle the late-inning duties from 1976-77, then be relegated to No. 2 when the Yankees picked up yet another free agent, Goose Gossage. And this despite the fact that Lyle had won the Cy Young Award in 1977 on the strength of his 13-5 mark with a 2.17 ERA and 27 saves. Such were the vicissitudes of life in the major leagues in general and under the reign of King George Steinbrenner in particular. Sparky feuded with his owner for much of that tumultuous season, then got the last word (sort of) by penning the best seller "The Bronx Zoo" with Peter Golenbock, detailing the antics of that curious 1978 aggregation besotted with equal parts of talent and eccentricity.

Of course, Lyle played as big (or bigger) a role with

1980-2001 Perez-Steele Hall of Fame Postcard Series.

Elston Howard's 1955 Bowman rookie card, and a pair of 1952 Topps.

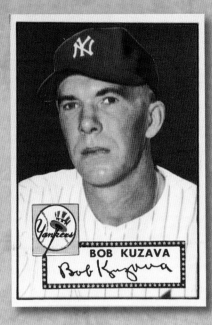

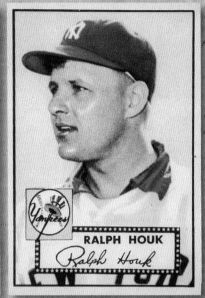

BOB KUZAVA

JOE PAGE

RALPH HOUK

JOE OSTROWSKI

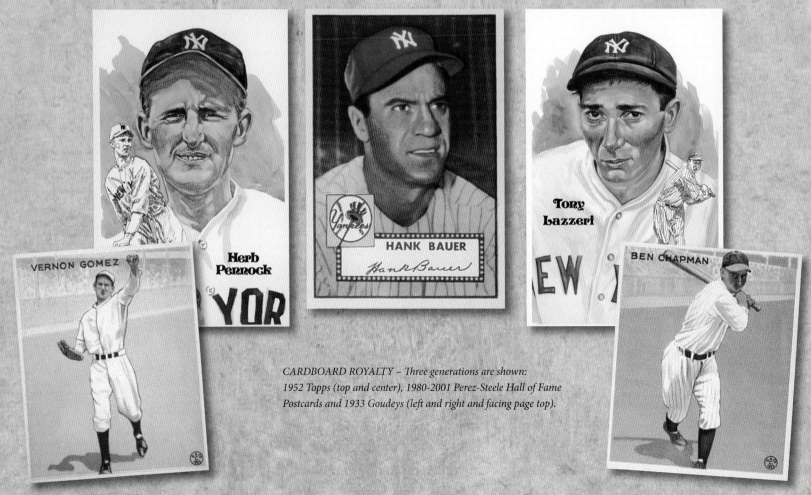

Herb Pennock

Tony Lazzeri

HANK BAUER

VERNON GOMEZ

BEN CHAPMAN

CARDBOARD ROYALTY – Three generations are shown:
1952 Topps (top and center), 1980-2001 Perez-Steele Hall of Fame
Postcards and 1933 Goudeys (left and right and facing page top).

the latter. Delivering a casket to the clubhouse, then planting himself inside while he awaited the start of a team meeting. As the lid creaked open, Lyle reportedly sat up and said in his finest Bela Lugosi mimicry: "How do you pitch to Brooks Robinson?"

Or scaring the exquisitely jumpy Phil Rizzuto with a Wolfman's mask on the an airplane, or sawing manager Bill Virdon's director's chair in half. Virdon looked like a guy who ought to be bedeviled by practical jokes like that, and so, naturally, Lyle complied.

Clearly the fun and games department never lacked for capable practitioners, but it was a different kind of chemistry that really created the biggest explosion in 1978. Ron Guidry had been a third-round draft choice by the team in 1971, and took a while to get to Yankee Stadium for good, but once he did there was pandemonium in the Bronx every time he took the mound that amazing year.

"Gator" had pitched a handful of innings in 1975-76, then blossomed into something special at age 26 the next year with a 16-7 mark. Five shutouts were included in that mix, and big things were expected as the spring of 1978 arrived.

That said, nobody could have anticipated what happened next. He won his first 13 games and created an electricity every time he took the mound that reminded fans of the Mark "The Bird" Fidrych days in 1976 or Vida Blue's incredible dominance in the first half of 1971. With a blazing fastball and a brutal slider he had picked up by watching Lyle, Guidry turned in perhaps the finest season for a starter since Denny McLain's 31-6 mark a decade before. At 25-3, with a 1.74 ERA, nine shutouts and 248 strikeouts, he was an easy (read unanimous) choice for the Cy Young, and barely missed the MVP Award behind Boston's Jim Rice.

Speaking of Boston, the 1978 season very nearly got away from

Red Ruffing premium.

the Yankees behind the continual thumping of Rice in Boston. But the Bosox folded down the stretch, and found themselves in a one-game playoff at Fenway against the Yankees. With the peripatetic Mike Torrez, signed as a free agent by the Red Sox after just under one full year in the Bronx, on the hill, Yankee shortstop Bucky Dent lifted a pop-fly three-run homer over the Green Monster, a blow that left Red Sox Nation retching and mewling for years to come.

Once again, the World Series wound up seeming anticlimactic as the Yankees rolled over the Dodgers in but six games yet again. It must have seemed as though it was time to start tossing around the "D" word once again after a 15-year hiatus. Not so fast, Buster.

The roster of the 1979 edition looked much like the 1977-78 champs, with an aging Tommy John added to the staff, and an even older Luis Tiant, but alas, Baltimore had re-emerged as a power once again, and the Yankees had to settle for fourth place in the AL East. Two unrelated events sealed the fate of a Yankee team that never really got untracked in 1979.

Burly Cliff Johnson was the team's designated hitter that year, but Goose Gossage wasn't included among the list of things he was designated to hit. The two wrestled in the locker room early in the year, and the ace reliever suffered a thumb injury that kept him on the sidelines for two months in the middle of the season. The eccentric Johnson was dealt to Cleveland, where he performed ably and somehow refrained from busting up any other teammates.

On August 2, Thurman Munson was killed when his private plane crashed as he was practicing takeoffs and landings from the Akron-Canton Regional Airport near his home. The loss of the 32-year-old

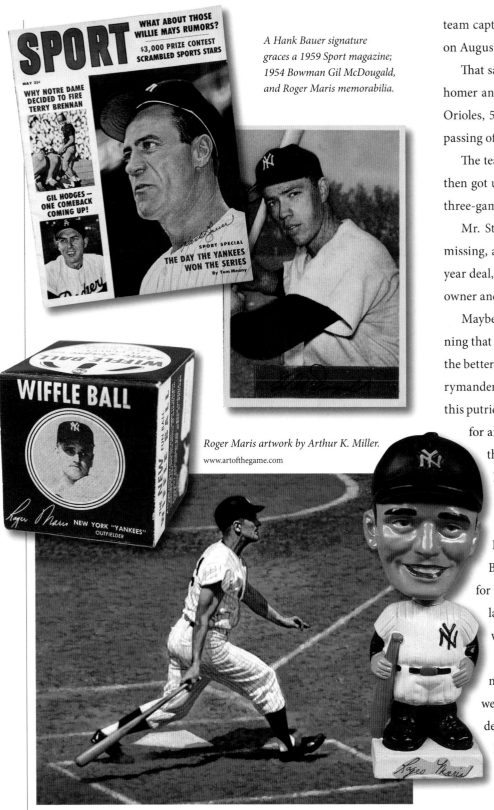

A Hank Bauer signature graces a 1959 Sport magazine; 1954 Bowman Gil McDougald, and Roger Maris memorabilia.

Roger Maris artwork by Arthur K. Miller.
www.artofthegame.com

team captain was devastating; the entire team attended his funeral on August 6, with Lou Piniella and Bobby Murcer giving eulogies.

That same night, Murcer drove in all five runs with a three-run homer and a ninth-inning, two-run single as the Yankees beat the Orioles, 5-4. It was Murcer's crowning moment as he marked the passing of his friend at one of the saddest times in Yankee history.

The team rallied back the following year, winning the East title, then got unceremoniously dumped by the Kansas City Royals in a three-game ALCS sweep.

Mr. Steinbrenner decided yet another piece to the puzzle was missing, and doled out $23 million to sign Dave Winfield to a 10-year deal, launching one of the epic love/hate relationships between owner and player in MLB history.

Maybe that rocky affair traces its roots to a decidedly icky beginning that wasn't Winfield's fault. The less said about the 1981 season the better: despoiled by a mid-season strike, the postseason was gerrymandered to include first and second-half winners, and through this putrid process the Yankees eventually emerged with what passes for an American League pennant. The Dodgers mercifully put that awful season to rest with a World Series drubbing of New York in six games. Finally a high point for the year: it was over.

And speaking of over, it was over for the Yankees, too. It would have been hard to predict at the time, but the Bronx Bombers would end up exiled from postseason play for 14 years; they did finish first in their division in 1994, but labor woes marred yet another season, and the postseason was canceled.

The musical chairs theme that was in force for the manager's spot would get a tryout for the wider roster as well over the next decade, with the less-than-modest results detailed above. This was the biggest part of Steinbrenner's learning curve of how to cope with free agency as he threw money at the oft-times unworthy. In 1986, a pitcher named Dennis Rasmussen had his finest season in the majors at

18-6, leading an odd pitching staff that had but one hurler recording double digits in wins, though they did have four nine-game winners. Ta da!

As many of the stalwarts from the championship years got old or got traded, new names turned up that didn't seem to have that same ring: Meacham, Pagliarulo, Pasqua and Tolleson. Other stop-gap measures brought the likes of Steve Sax and Danny Tartabull to Yankee Stadium, the former who suffered for a time with a form of "Steve Blass disease," a curious inability at times to make the throw to first base from the environs of second base, and the latter who had a couple of good seasons after accepting $5 million in free-agent largesse before fading away.

Rickey Henderson even made an appearance on Broadway, so to speak, coming to New York in 1985 near the peak of his Hall-of-Fame career as he held dual titles as the fastest man and the loosest lip in MLB.

Henderson scored 276 runs and stole 167 bases in his first two years, the kind of production that you would have thought would have immediately earned him a plaque in Monument Park, but he lasted barely more than four seasons before being shipped back to Oakland.

Luis Arroyo souvenir pin.

Arguably the greatest leadoff hitter of all time, Henderson's ascendancy in baseball was perfectly timed with two events that altered the way fans looked at the game's statistics. Fantasy baseball leagues were coming into vogue in the 1980s at the same time as a heightened (and more sophisticated) interpretation of stats was being championed by followers of the Society for American Baseball Research (SABR). To these folks, Henderson's unique array of talents – walks, home run power, runs scored and stolen bases – propelled him into the pantheon of the game's elite. As Henderson might have put it, "Rickey belongs there."

His phenomenal numbers aside, those Yankee squads wound up in second place in 1985-86, and further down the pike after that, and as every baseball fan knows, that doesn't make it in New York.

The inability to return to the postseason was especially irksome for the team's marquee player, Don Mattingly, who ultimately earned the quaint nickname "Donnie Baseball," and not just because "Mr. October" was already taken.

The purest hitter in the game never got to the World Series, having extraordinary timing at bat and something less than that in terms of his career. A beloved Yankee virtually from his first full season,

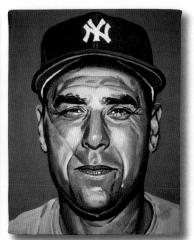

Andy Jurinko artwork (left to right) of Gil McDougald, Elston Howard, Vic Raschi and Eddie Lopat.

which included a rare Yankee batting title (.343), his 14-year career neatly matched the longest World Series drought in team history.

And just to rub it in a bit, the Yankees did sample postseason play in 1995, Year No. 2 of MLB's embrace of a Wild-Card format. Mattingly hardly could have done more, batting .417 and knocking in six runs, but the Wild Card Yanks were defeated in five games by the Seattle Mariners, aided in large part by the best player in the game, Ken Griffey Jr., who hit five homers and logged nine RBIs in the series.

A bad back that had dogged Mattingly for several years drove him out of the game after that bittersweet ending, which history would nudge even more as the final dynasty of the old millennium (and the first of the new one) would begin just as "Donnie Baseball" stepped away.

With newly installed manager Joe Torre at the helm, a team composed of by-now top-shelf veteran stars (Bernie Williams, Paul O'Neill, and Wade Boggs), a supporting cast of aging All-Stars (Ruben Sierra, Darryl Strawberry, Tim Raines and Cecil Fielder) proved to be

"Poosh 'Em Up" Tony Lazzeri and two Yankee heartaches: Al Giofriddo robs DiMaggio in the 1947 Series and Sandy Amoros saves Game Seven for the Bums in '55.
Andy Jurinko artwork.

www.goodsportsart.com

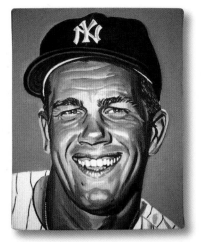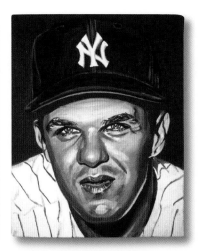

Andy Jurinko artwork of Tony Kubek, Joe Collins, Moose Skowron and Bob Turley.

a formidable mix, especially with the addition of a rookie.

Derek Jeter wowed Yankee fans from the start, and his 1996 campaign, as a 21-year-old rookie at a vitally important defensive position, was nothing short of amazing. The baseball writers agreed, making him the Rookie of the Year, and thus the legend was born.

Comparing dynasties is tough, for the same reason that comparing gals you've dated is tough: way too many variables to take into account. That said, the Torre-led, Jeter-captained aggregation would push its way into the record books, with 12 consecutive post-season appearances, six American League pennants and four World Series crowns. Only in New York could that seem like a disappointment, especially the "no trips to the Fall Classic after 2003" part.

Jeter was front and center through all of it, Torre likewise, and by 1998 the combination of an imposing, unflappable day-to-day lineup, five starters who might have been aces on any number of other teams and an other-worldly reliever added up to a major-league record 114 wins and an 11-2 postseason buzz saw through the playoffs and World Series. Suddenly, cries of "Break up the Yankees" that hadn't been heard for nearly a half-century were popping up throughout the land.

That club, with Jorge Posada (c), Tino Martinez (1b), Chuck Knoblauch (2b), Jeter (ss), Scott Brosius (3b) and Williams, O'Neill and Chad Curtis in the outfield and a staff of Andy Pettitte, David

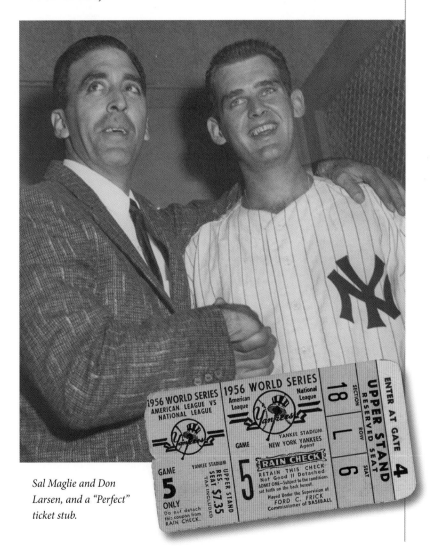

Sal Maglie and Don Larsen, and a "Perfect" ticket stub.

Cone, David Wells, Hideki Irabu and Orlando Hernandez handled innings 1-8 about as easily as any team in baseball history, and Mariano Rivera would stroll in 36 times to take care of the ninth.

All in all, a happy time to be in the Bronx. The club just missed drawing 3 million fans, a figure it would then sail past the next year; by 2005, a total of 4 million would be the benchmark.

Few teams can win 16 fewer games from one year to the next and maintain their previous spot in the standings, but the 1999 team managed that nicely, and even upped the postseason efficiency to 11-1. They had even added a Hall of Fame pitcher (or should we say another one) to the staff: Roger Clemens, although the staff ERA of 4.13 was hardly befitting a ball club with 98 wins. Only later would we find out that, uh, chemically enhanced offensive numbers had made it tough for moundsmen as the millennium came to a close.

The next year the win total fell to 87, but that still was good enough to yield an East Division crown, which led to a ho-hum 11-5 postseason and a World Series win of particular relish: a triumph over their rivals from Queens, the Mets, in the first Subway Series since 1956.

The 2001 edition added more firepower with the exciting young-

When Satchel came to The Stadium.
Photo courtesy of Hunt Auctions

Rick Cerone souvenir button. (David Spindel Collection)

 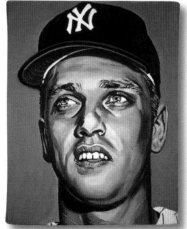

Andy Jurinko artwork of Don Larsen and Roger Maris (above) Roger Clemens (right) and Jason Giambi on facing page. Steve Jacobson photos

ster Alfonso Soriano at second base, along with a pretty fair country pitcher in Mike Mussina, who came by way of Baltimore bringing his 137 wins with him. By the time this book went to print, he would have essentially doubled that number in eight impressive seasons at Yankee Stadium. But the team lost a squeaker to the Arizona Diamondbacks in a seven-game World Series, and for the first time there seemed to be cracks in the veneer.

In 2002, they wouldn't even get to the World Series, losing in the ALCS to the California Angels; a 101-61 season in 2003 would end with a World Series drubbing in six games at the fins, er, hands of the Florida Marlins, a team with a payroll just a fraction of the Yankees' total. Could it get worse?

Yep. From 2004-07, three AL East titles and a Wild Card berth (2007) would produce three early exits from postseason play, most notably an ALCS tank job in 2004 when their hated rivals, the Boston Red Sox, came back from a three games to none deficit to send the Yankees home and propel the Sox on to their first World Series win in quite some time. Eighty-six years, to be exact, to a time when that team had enjoyed the services of the last great two-way player, Babe Ruth.

This was not the way Steinbrenner had drawn it up. Alex Rodriguez, the highest-paid player in this particular quadrant of the universe, arrived in Gotham in 2004, as the game's first $22-million a year man, but The Boss would be forced to relearn once again about that old bromide of "money isn't everything."

And Rodriguez even had help, all to no avail, at least in the post-season, anyway. Slugger Jason Giambi had been signed as a free agent after the 2001 season, all $120 million worth (seven-year contract), and he didn't disappoint either, with matching 41-homer seasons his first two in New York. Another basher, Gary Sheffield, arrived in

2004 and also delivered handsomely – at least until injury felled him in 2006 – but still no happy ending.

There was another Cy Young hurler brought on board – Randy Johnson in 2005 – and more trades or free agency brought other All-Stars (Johnny Damon and Bobby Abreu) and home-grown talent as well (Robinson Cano), and even a great star imported from Japan in Hideki Matsui, but there was something that was starting to become apparent, if entirely unwelcome.

As the Yankees' payroll soared past $200 million annually, many an American League fan had despaired that the worst fears about big-market vs. small-market teams in Major League Baseball were coming true. When the Yankees won four World Series in a five-year span, the naysayers moaned that the top prize in the game was there for the taking by the team with the dough to take it.

True enough, perhaps, but it's also becoming ever more apparent that having a gargantuan payroll can often get you into the playoffs (though no guarantee even there), but after that you're on your own. While MLB payrolls have reached head-spinning levels over the past decade, there have been enough instances of sporadic and even reasonably consistent success from some of the smaller-market ball clubs that simply wagging your finger at the evil Yankees probably isn't as satisfying in 2008 as it might have been in 1960.

Just ask the Tampa Bay Devil Rays, or the Minnesota Twins. Yankees fans wound up saying farewell to their beloved Stadium and then endured the anguish of watching its demolition, all without the decency of an October sayonara at the World Series, or even in the playoffs, for that matter.

That's hardly the way it was supposed to end for "The House that Ruth Built."

"Yankee Stadium Triumph" by Bill Purdom. www.goodsportsart.com

Chapter 10

Reggie, Thurm and Donnie Baseball

From 1932 to 1964 – a span of 33 seasons – the New York Yankees won 23 pennants and 17 World Series crowns. From 1965 to 1995 – a span of 31 seasons – the Yankees won three pennants and two World Series titles. For older fans accustomed to watching championship baseball in October, the winding down of the millennium proved to be a difficult period indeed.

Thurman Munson and Reggie Jackson were at the center of those two World Series wins in 1977-78; Don Mattingly carried the Yankee banner with an unusual dignity and stature for 14 years from 1982-95. It's the cruelest of ironies that it was also the longest stretch without a World Series appearance since Babe Ruth signed on the dotted line. Toward the end of Mattingly's career in 1994, the club was in first place when the strike came along, leading eventually to the cancelation of the World Series. Once he retired, the team would win three in four seasons.

It was that commitment to getting the team back into the postseason that prompted George Steinbrenner to bring Reggie Jackson

1980-2001 Perez-Steele Hall of Fame Postcard Series.

to New York in 1977 by way of a $2.96 million contract that sounded like a lot of money at the time. The Yankees had finally reached the World Series in 1976 after an 11-year drought, but had been promptly dispatched in four games by Cincinnati's Big Red Machine.

The Boss wanted to win a World Series, not just show up for it, and he saw Jackson as the final piece of the puzzle. Jackson had not been anointed with the "Mr. October" tag line just yet, but that would come soon enough.

The irascible Reggie, already a major star with two home run crowns and three World Series rings on his resume, wasted no time in bumping up against an old rival, manager Billy Martin. Reggie had helped dump Martin's scrappy Detroit Tigers club from the playoffs in 1972, and Billy rarely forgave or forgot. "I hate him,"

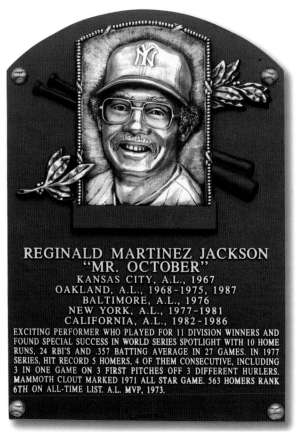

Reggie's Hall of Fame hardware – better than a candy bar.
National Baseball Hall of Fame and Library, Cooperstown, N.Y.

Reggie was quoted as saying, "but if I played for him, I'd probably love him." That's not exactly how it worked out.

Jackson was the first black superstar to play in New York, and the import of that should hardly be lost on anyone familiar with the exaggerated importance of everything that goes on in The Big Apple.

It was also the tumultuous 1970s, with the racial tension of a decade earlier now put to simmer, but the combination of that fact and the huge pile of money (for the times) thrown at him put him in a pressurized situation like no other.

It's probably too simplistic to say that three swings made Reggie Jackson, since he almost certainly would still have made his way to Cooperstown without that three-homer dream sequence in the 1977 World Series. But without them, he wouldn't have been Reggie. And for Jackson, that's always going to be the point.

With an apartment on Fifth Avenue and a huge Rolls Royce, Jackson cut a dashing figure on New York's tony Upper East Side. "He would walk around his neighborhood and walk into an art gallery and admire a Picasso and move on," famed author Roger Kahn said of Jackson in an interview in 2003 as he promoted his new book, "October Men." "I don't know how many blacks had ever lived in that neighborhood before."

And while it was an infamous comment (fairly attributed or not) about his being "the straw that stirs the drink" that got him in hot water with teammates virtually from the start of the 1977 campaign, Kahn offers the view that it was an accurate assessment.

"It turned out that it was Reggie," Kahn said with finality. "In 1976, the Yankees won, and that was Martin's triumphant return to the team that had banished him in the 1950s. I was at the World Series, and the Big Red Machine was really just a much better club. Martin stopped the running game when he saw Johnny Bench's arm. And the Reds swept."

It was that jarring experience that sent Steinbrenner looking westward to Oakland at the dawn of free agency. "And one thing Reggie said when he was looking to make a deal with the Yankees was that no team with Reggie Jackson would ever be humiliated like that in the World Series. And no team with Reggie Jackson ever was," said Kahn.

Jackson's braggadocio was hardly ever challenged after the Game Six heroics in the 1977 Series. "I truly believed that I was the best in those situations. I wanted everything to be right for the opposition," Jackson said when asked about his "Mr. October" reputation. "I wanted the opposing pitcher to feel very confident and come after me. I honestly felt that I was going to capitalize on the situation and win."

Collectors Corner: Few players were ever better suited – or embraced more fervently – the arcane world of sports collectibles than did Reggie. Almost from the start of the hobby boom in the 1980s, Jackson was in the thick of it at card shows, first as an autograph guest but eventually as an avid collector in his own right. And of his own cards.

By 2001, he owned nearly 300 of his rookie cards, though he had lost perhaps five dozen or so in a fire at his home several years earlier. The initial idea was reportedly to accumulate 563 of those 1969 Topps cards, one for every home run in his career, and autograph each one. The fire and the increased awareness from dealers that Jackson was on a quest helped put the kibosh on that grand idea. "I'll give a whole bunch to my daughter (age 18), sell some and give the money away to my charity. I give them away to people sometimes."

Inducted into the Hall of Fame in 1993, Jackson saw another boost in his persona a couple of years later as the Yankees began their amazing run of four World Series titles in five years. Jackson noted the undeniable link.

"Sooner or later, I know that I will be at the pinnacle in the autograph business, because of the Yankees, because of New York, because of Reggie Jackson, because of my World Series," he continued.

"Not necessarily because I was the best player, though there's an argument for that. The Yankees success over the last five years has added to my mystique, without a doubt. The aura and presence gets larger and bigger and more mythic."

Just think of it: a more mythic Mr. October.

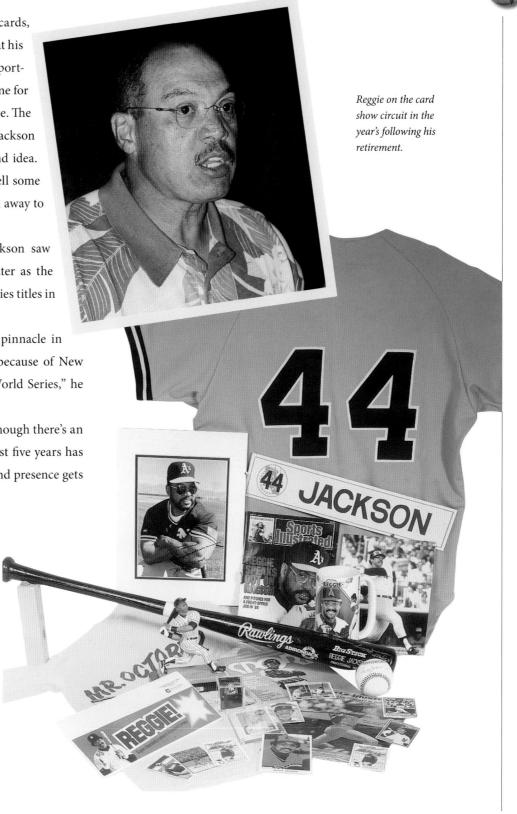

Reggie on the card show circuit in the year's following his retirement.

The self-anointed "straw that stirs the drink" began doing just that shortly after arriving in the Big Apple in 1977, and the endorsement goodies – including that oft-described vile candy bar – were not far behind.

Reggie may have been the final puzzle piece that helped push the Yankees over the top in their two World Championships in 1977-78, but diehard Yankee fans will point to Thurman Munson as the heart and soul of those gritty Yankee teams of the 1970s.

For Munson's legion of supporters, his death at age 32 from a plane crash cut short a career that might have led to Cooperstown; those with a more objective perspective might conclude that his trajectory was never quite to that level.

Lost in the debate is the realization that careers can be measured in other ways than simply raw statistics, and it is there that the Yankees' first captain since Lou Gehrig shines. He was an inspiration to teammates and fans alike, bringing a fierce competitiveness to a ball club that hadn't finished closer than 20 games out of first place since the last pennant in 1964.

The team quietly pushed its way back into American League contention in 1974-75 before breaking through to win the pennant in 1976 behind a remarkable MVP season from Munson.

Regarded as a lethal clutch hitter, Munson had turned in a stellar 1975 season, including reaching an unusual statistical threshold: driving in more than 100 runs with only 12 home runs (and batting .318). In all, he topped the .300 mark five times in his 11-year career, which included seven All-Star selections.

For nearly 30 years since his death on Aug. 2, 1979, the stall that housed Munson's locker remains untouched – only a few feet away from the current captain, Derek Jeter. The metal locker is where it belongs: in Cooperstown.

But Munson isn't there, and by all indications not likely to be in the near-term future. Marty Appel, who wrote the foreword for this book, collaborated with Munson on his autobiography in 1978 and followed it up with

"Munson" by Arthur K. Miller; plus Reggie on the cover of Baseball Illustrated.

Thurman Munson cap and signed ball. (David Spindel Collection)

"Munson: The Life and Death of a Yankee Captain (Doubleday)," slated for release in the spring of 2009. No greater Munson fan can be found, and even he doesn't quibble with the great backstop falling short of immortal status.

"You could easily fill up a plaque with all his accomplishments, but his career was simply too short," Appel said. "And those who saw him play every day knew that his career had already peaked. His best years were behind him."

Which hardly deters Munson's faithful followers. "When I went back to games to take photos for my book, I saw lots of grown men, most of them middle-aged and overweight, wearing Thurman Munson jerseys to Yankee Stadium," Appel continued. "That's just the kind of guy Munson was – he touched working-class people. If Thurman could witness that scene, it would certainly make him smile."

Thurman Munson's 1976 MVP Award brought $126,500 at the 2008 All-Star Auction in New York City.

Courtesy Hunt Auctions

Through much of the 1980s, despite the Yankees' lackluster placement in the standings every year, Don Mattingly was perhaps the marquee player in the game. With six All-Star nods, nine Gold Gloves, three Silver Sluggers, a batting title and the 1985 American League MVP Award, Cooperstown appeared to be little more than a formality. But back troubles that flared up in 1990 would rob him of that ultimate honor, leaving "The Hit Man" arguably the most revered Yankee player in history not to be assigned HOF status.

Unlike in the case of Munson, the debate about Mattingly's HOF worthiness is a bit more complicated and intense, largely because of one of those statistical peculiarities that so bedevil the Hall-of-Fame voting process and ignite Hot Stove League chatter ad infinitum.

Mattingly's numbers are virtually identical to Kirby Puckett's, and both careers neatly coincided roughly from 1984-95. The Hot

"Donnie Baseball," certainly one of the most beloved Yankees of the modern era, is shown above left in original artwork by Dan Gardiner and above in a signed photograph. Photo from the David Spindel Collection
At left is Mattingly's 1993 Score Select card.

Stove League wrangle emanates from jousting about the relative importance of World Series heroics (Puckett had plenty, Mattingly zero), but the reality is that there is no discernible difference in assessing the two careers.

But circumstances aside from raw numbers have contributed to Puckett's first-ballot election and Mattingly's exclusion. With his first year of eligibility, Donnie Baseball got 28 percent of the vote – hardly a harbinger of hopeful HOF chances – and quickly plummeted to about half of that in the following votes. There's essentially no precedent for a player halfway through his BBWAA voting eligibility bringing those kinds of numbers up to the 75 percent needed for election.

It seems like that he will have to await his turn with the Veterans Committee, hoping that his contemporaries and other HOFers will look more kindly on his career, perhaps remembering that for much of the 1980s, he was the biggest name in baseball. There are a whole lot of guys enshrined in Cooperstown who can't make that claim.

And casual fans may not be aware that Mattingly also played a huge role in the card collecting hobby in the 1980s as well. As a batting champ in just his first full season at age 23, he captivated a throng of card collectors eager for a hero from their own generation to compete with the dusty lineup from earlier eras.

Mattingly helped launch the idea – for good or ill, depending upon your view – that baseball cards fresh off the presses could be valuable (meaning expensive), just like their older counterparts. This

Mattingly poses with Puckett above; also shown, his 1984 Donruss rookie card, once one of the hottest cards in the hobby.

giddy concept helped reshape the whole hobby as tens of thousands of new "collectors" stepped gleefully into the arena hoping that buying a case of baseball cards was a good move for augmenting junior's college fund.

That the investment strategy turned out to be flawed – the investment bubble would burst, coincidentally at just about the same time that Mattingly's back was tanking – or that Donnie Baseball's sharp decline after 1990 torpedoed at least his near-term HOF chances, would hardly detract from his historical impact.

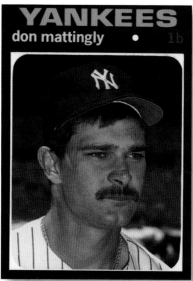

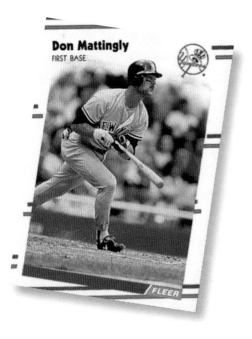

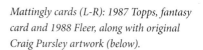

Mattingly cards (L-R): 1987 Topps, fantasy card and 1988 Fleer, along with original Craig Pursley artwork (below).

Pen and ink artwork by T.S. O'Connell; 1980 (Reggie) and 1991 Topps cards are shown.

Derek Jeter artwork by James Fiorentino. www.jamesfiorentino.com

Chapter 11

Jeter

"*Derek Jeter, '53*" *by James Fiorentino*
www.goodsportsart.com

Derek Jeter is the kind of guy who can make you believe in something called "The Yankee Mystique," whether you are inclined to such musings or not. The captain of the Yankees is young, handsome, single, headed for the Hall of Fame with a fistful of World Series rings and just generally the kind of man that every youngster in America would like to grow up to be. The oldsters are reasonably enamored of the lifestyle too, even if it may be a tad too late to be dreaming about playing shortstop for the Yankees.

That's precisely what Derek Sanderson Jeter has done for the last 13 years, and he's done it in a fashion that's certain to plant him among the all-time greats at his position.

He's also the heir apparent in a line of regal succession that traces all the way back to Babe Ruth and the opening of Yankee Stadium in 1923. Yankee Royalty can be debated, especially about questions of designating kings, princes and the like (no queens yet), but clearly Jeter belongs in that distinguished family tree of Ruth, Gehrig, DiMaggio, Mantle, Berra, Ford, Rizzuto, Jackson, Mattingly, and now Rodriguez.

While the parameters of nobility have to be somewhat malleable, playing your whole career in the Big Apple is a nice plus that worked wonders for most of the Yankees Royal Family. In Jeter's case, playing the most important position in the infield with Gold Glove efficiency and Sports Center-friendly elan doesn't hurt either.

That Yankee captaincy thing is a big plus, too. As the 2008 campaign neared it's unseemly (for the Yankees) finish, Jeter already has all his Cooperstown credentials neatly organized and in place: .316 lifetime average, more than 2,500 hits, more than 200 homers and pushing 1,500 runs scored.

If that weren't enough (but it is), there are also things like nine All-Star selections, three Gold Gloves, two Silver Slugger awards,

Steve Jacobson photo (top); Al Bello/Allsport photo (bottom).

Shortstop Derek Jeter hits the ball during a playoff game against the Baltimore Orioles on Oct. 9, 1996 The Yankees won the game, 5-4.

the 2000 World Series MVP Award, 2000 Babe Ruth Award, and his 1996 Rookie-of-the-Year nod.

But just as Hall-of-Fame selection is about more than just numbers, so too is reaching that upper echelon in the hearts of Yankee fans. Like the game itself, it ultimately becomes about winning, and Jeter's managed that to a degree far beyond any of his contemporaries and right up there in the same league as his storied Gotham ancestors.

Until the 2008 season, Jeter could have been forgiven if he just sort of assumed that playing in the postseason is some kind of birthright. The Yankees qualified for the postseason in some fashion or other (usually with an AL Eastern Division title) every year of his career from 1995-2007, and won six pennants and four World Series to boot.

All of which totals up to a fairy tale life made even bigger and more colossal by the bright lights of Broadway, literally and figuratively. The most eligible bachelor in the most important city in the world finds himself dating models and actresses, endorsing products, signing autographs and just generally living the life of The King of New York.

And Jeter has much else in common with the likes of Mickey Mantle in the almost eerie parallel conjured up by Jeter's time as reigning superstar and the arrival in of teammate Alex Rodriguez in 2004. Mantle faced something similar when, at the peak of his remarkable career, the team added a new name to the roster in 1960: Roger Maris.

Maris quickly won two Most Valuable Player Awards, a feat that Rodriguez accomplished in 2005 and 2007 (he had an earlier MVP in 2003, his last year as a Texas Ranger). And just like in the case of the Mantle/Maris history, something peculiar but probably predictable happened. The arrival of the newcomer gave the Yankee fans a greater appreciation of the player who had so long been in their midst.

Thus was the legend of the Captain bolstered and extended, even as the Yankees stumbled repeatedly in the postseason. Serious fans were tough on the new guy, especially in what seemed like a stark contrast to their embrace of Jeter.

Almost from the start Jeter seemed to have an understanding and appreciation of the link to those storied players from so many earlier decades, and he most tellingly would offer props to many of them that he encountered at the Stadium. "One of the best things about playing for the Yankees is how accessible former Yankee players are," Jeter said in a 1999 interview.

"We have people working with us in spring training who are living legends, and we can talk to them about anything. And they give us a lot of time."

One of the things they may not discuss is the phenomenal money that permeates the modern game, and quite fairly permeates Jeter's bankbook as well. In his 13 full seasons he's pocketed about $160 million-plus in salary from George Steinbrenner,

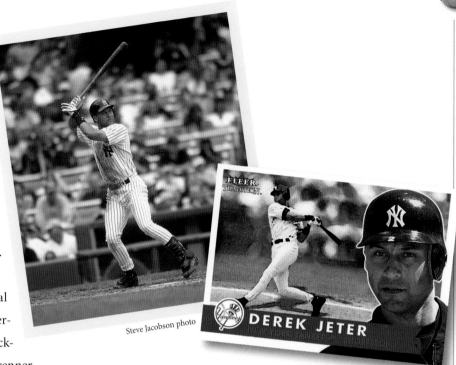

Steve Jacobson photo

2001 Fleer Tradition

"Yankee Two Treasure" by Bill Williams. www.goodsportsart.com

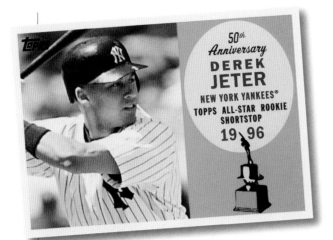

The Topps Rookie All-Star subset traces its roots back to 1960.

but given the whirring turnstiles of more than 4 million fans every year, you have to poke around a bit to find fans convinced that Jeter was overpaid.

And besides, despite that stratospheric pay scale and exalted status in the Big Apple, there is a genuine sense of Jeter's humility in an age when that's a rare commodity with zillionaire athletes.

"Derek is the true ambassador of the game," said Chris Amoroso, executive VP of Steiner Sports, which is the exclusive provider of Jeter-signed memorabilia. "I've had more players from other teams say they love Derek and they would take him to start their team. You're talking about his rivals."

One of Amoroso's rivals, Scott Widelitz of Mounted Memories, offered similar sentiments about Jeter, but with a twist. "Jeter's been called a likable Joe DiMaggio. As nice as he is, and as politically correct as he is and as gracious as he is, he's also protective of 'Derek Jeter' and of who he lets in, and that's the way DiMaggio was."

And just like The Yankee Clipper, Jeter engenders that kind of fan devotion by parlaying his offensive skills with a flair for the defensive side of things. While Joe D would be limited to grainy black-and-white film clips that turned up in newsreels before the Saturday matinee, Jeter is one of the darlings of the modern cable television age. His headlong dashes into the stands pursuing foul balls or a patented leaping throw from deep in the hole at shortstop have become a staple for ESPN watchers.

"I think offense is overrated," Jeter intoned in that interview during the 1999 season. "Right now, when you turn on sports, the first thing you see are home runs, followed by big hits. So it's obvious that's what the fans want to see. But if you're a critical observer of the game, you'll notice the defensive plays that really save a game or turn a game around."

In fairness to the ESPN types, the cable TV icon does provide a good deal of attention to the defensive side with its daily top plays. "I don't care how many home runs you hit or how many RBIs you have, if you're out in the field giving runs away, you're not helping the team," Jeter continued. "I think players focus on defense, and I think managers look for defense. I think defense is the first thing you should think about."

It's that kind of attitude, which by virtually all accounts seems genuine, that would seem to set Jeter apart from many of his contemporaries. And there's something else that sets him apart, though not as much as you might think.

Jeter, with a black father and a white mother, would seem to be the post-racial bookend for the new President of the United States with similar parental lineage. Though his light-skinned complexion no doubt plays a role, Jeter truly seems to be beyond that tired old saga of defining someone first and foremost by the color of their skin. The affection of generation of Yankee fans for Jeter is as genuine as it is nearly universal. And it's clearly a two-way street.

"New York is the greatest city in the world, the greatest place for an athlete, and I don't know why anyone wouldn't want to play here," he said with finality.

And by "here," he presumably meant the new Yankee Stadium. Jeter and the monuments and plaques outside the center field wall made the short trip to the new facility in the spring of 2009. Eventually, he'll have his own monument, though Yankee fans are in no hurry for that one.

DEREK JETER

SHORTSTOP
DEREK JETER

2001 Topps Heritage cards of the captain.
photo by Steve Jacobson

Steve Jacobson photo

Chapter 12

A-Rod by the Numbers

Baseball is a game ruled by numbers, even at its most elemental level. Three strikes. Four balls. Nine innings. The very jargon of the game depends upon them. It's a 3-2 count, two outs, two men on. The measure of the game demands them: .300 batting average, 20 wins, 500 home runs, 3,000 hits. Rule the numbers and you rule the game. Or so it should seem.

Alex Rodriguez is a man of mind-bending talent but even more mind-boggling numbers. It says here that he's managed to do something that no ballplayer has ever done before: his numbers are too good, too other worldly, too imposing – so much so that they've propelled him to a spot that is awash with the cruelest of contradictions. He's so good that nobody seems to truly appreciate how good he is. Is that like Yogi's apocryphal restaurant that's so busy that no one goes there anymore?

As the 2008 campaign came to a close, A-Rod had his .306 lifetime average, 552 home runs, more than 1,600 RBIs and a similar number of runs scored. These are numbers compiled in essentially 13 full seasons and brief call-ups in two others. Using that lucky number 13,

he has averaged 40 home runs per season and about 124 runs and 124 RBIs per. So his average has essentially been an MVP season for most anybody else. He has three of those awards, but if you believe the numbers, he might have earned a dozen.

His signing with the Yankees in 2004 prompted an unusual event: a player who might be anointed the best in the game changes defensive position in mid-

RODRIGUEZ, NEW YORK - AMERICANS

2004 Topps Cracker Jack

career. Rodriguez, noting that the club had a pretty fair country shortstop already well entrenched at Yankee Stadium in his then-pal Derek Jeter, agreed to move to third base.

A-Rod fans would presumably describe that as a selfless act from a star player rarely accused of altruism; more-cynical types might characterize it as an unavoidable accommodation to allow for the

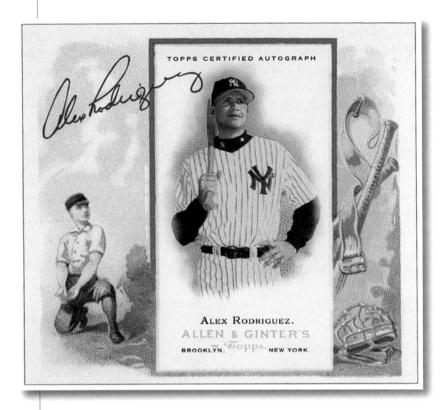

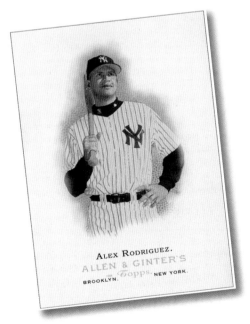

2006 Topps Allen & Ginter's cards, including an autographed version at the top of the page.

monetary rewards that were offered by Mr. Steinbrenner. He could even be given the benefit of the doubt and the decision to move to third could be reasonably placed on the altar of A-Rod's desire to play in a World Series, which by definition is accorded greater probability for a third baseman in New York than for a shortstop in Arlington, Texas.

But however you assess his motivations, the reality is that what would have been a glaring, dare we say oppressive spotlight upon debuting in New York with many millions tucked away in his bank book was made all the more onerous with the defensive change.

And there were plenty of signs in that first tumultuous season in the Big Apple that even the seemingly impervious A-Rod could have his feathers ruffled, including defensive lapses that usually infuriated fans in the Bronx and manager Joe Torre as well. Still, he was posting offensive numbers that would have been thrilling for mere mortal ballplayers, and by Year No. 2 he had returned to his top-season form. The naysayers were put at bay for the moment, but hardly silenced. They would perhaps not-so-patiently await other moments to take note that the mega-millionaire in their midst was somehow still a disappointment, gaudy statistics notwithstanding.

It is the curse that comes with the dough, and A-Rod is the poster child of the modern, super-wealthy baseball player in an age when the scale of the game makes him more removed from the fans who pay the freight than any who came before him. The Hall of Famers from the 1950s and 1960s whose numbers he has dwarfed used to go home in the winter and work at the local bank or the used-car dealership to make ends meet. These days, the bankers come to A-Rod, who, coincidentally, owns a Mercedes-Benz dealership in League City, Texas.

There are few fraternities as tightly knit as professional athletes who perform at the highest level, and so Alex Rodriguez and Brooks Robinson would find much in common should they one day have adjoining rocking chairs on the veranda of the Hotel Otesaga in Cooperstown, but in real down-and-dirty economics, Brooksie would have more in common with the youngsters pestering them both for autographs than he would with A-Rod. Money is the ultimate determining factor in placing us comfortably among our peers.

And he has done all this by the time he's reached the ripe old age of 33. If he had decided to chuck it all a couple of years ago and move to Tahiti, he still would have been guaranteed a spot in Cooperstown; heck, you can make a good case that he would have been induction-worthy without playing so much as one day after his 30th birthday.

Of course, had he opted to take up painting by the numbers and sipping sangria on a tropical island for the rest of his days, he would have left perhaps a quarter of a billion dollars on the table. Obviously, that would be unthinkable, but there are other forces aside from a $27 million paycheck annually that keep him in the ball game.

For one, he would like to play in the World Series. That's probably as understated as the man himself. He needs to play in a World Series. More than that, he needs to play in a World Series and play very well in it if and when the time comes, thank you.

After 13 full-time seasons, he has yet to set foot on baseball's grandest stage, a peculiarity in his record that presumably poses as much of an aggravation as anything can for a guy in his particular tax bracket. Only A-Rod knows the extent to which he is bothered by this albatross, but for legions of fans and sportswriters it threatens to overshadow everything else. In a team game that writes its golden history in the collective glory of winning the World Series, failing to even get there is a mortal sin. Getting there and failing to win it, that's a venial sin.

And it makes no matter that the Catholic church no longer deals with that antiquated bit of ecclesiastical effluvium: for fans accustomed to a world where we only pay attention to the top of the pyramid, playing in the World Series is a must.

For the more cerebral baseball enthusiast, there's some tacit acknowledgement that fate can play a pretty significant role in determining such things. "The Greatest Hitter Who Ever Lived," as Ted Williams always hoped people would refer to him, played his whole career on a Red Sox club that only rarely could measure up to their

2005 Topps Turkey Red (left) and his 2008 Topps regular-issue card (below).

hated rivals the Yankees, and thus Williams played in but one World Series, and he performed poorly in that one.

A-Rod's first five full seasons were with Seattle as he quickly blossomed into the top shortstop in the game. When his crack at free agency came following the end of the 2000 season, he ended up signing a 10-year contract with the Texas Rangers worth a reported $252 million dollars. This may have marked the beginning of the baseball world's bipolar love/hate relationship with its best player.

Heading south to the cozy, homer-friendly Ballpark in Arlington was cited as evidence that Rodriguez placed tawdry things like huge piles of dough ahead of a self-avowed reverence for winning. One of the least-successful teams in MLB history, the Rangers had never been to the World Series since their slap-dash incarnation in 1961 as the "new" Washington Senators after the "old" ones skedaddled to Minnesota.

And they never did in the mere three years that Rodriguez stayed there, though it was hardly his fault that they did not. Through the heart of the 2001-03 era that has since been tainted by the apparent widespread application of steroids to boost power numbers, A-Rod averaged 52 home runs and 132 RBIs per year.

It is fascinating to note that despite the steroid and human growth hormone revelations that occurred after 2004, Rodriguez escaped largely unscathed despite his spectacular production.

He also emerged from his banishment after the 2003 season, ending up as a member of the Yankees. It seemed at the time like a logical place for him to take the next chapter of his career: the best player in the game arrives at the most successful franchise. But it was never that simple, or thus far, with a typical storybook ending.

After the 2003 season, the Rangers' crack management team decided to unload their $252-million man, apparently doing a little ex post facto math and realizing that they couldn't afford their star player. A deal with the Red Sox seemed all but finalized before the Players Association nixed it because it included a voluntary reduction in salary by Rodriguez, hardly a precedent that the association wanted to see put into play. In February, the Yankees stepped up to the plate and completed a swap with the Rangers, with Rodriguez heading north in exchange for Alfonso Soriano and that charming baseball oddity the "player to be named later."

That component of the deal (Joaquin Arias) probably wasn't as vital to the completion as the agreement that the Rangers would pay $67 million of the $179 million left on that whopping contract they had doled out three years before. The Texas Rangers' long and well-deserved reputation for laughable front-office malfeasance was burnished yet again.

And if A-Rod struggled a bit in his first season in New York (36 homers and 106 RBIs, which constitutes struggling by his lofty standards), he quickly put the muzzle to his critics in 2005 with his second of three MVP seasons. With 48 home runs and 130 driven in to go with a shiny .321 batting average, it was pretty clear that his was a Yankee Stadium-worthy talent, even if the fans still seemed more enamored of their shortstop Captain Jeter.

Aside from the occasional defensive misadventure at third, finding bona fide criticism points about Rodriguez would seem to be a challenging undertaking. He is a fine base runner, putting up stolen base totals that would have caused a fuss for anybody else, including a career-high 46 in 1998 for Seattle.

And, of course, for the hyper-critical, there are those irksome strikeouts, which come in substantial but hardly worrisome bunches. When you have a guy averaging about 130 RBIs per season, it might seem like a stretch to moan about him whiffing at about the same frequency. Complaining about A-Rod's penchant for striking out seems to me akin to lamenting that Ashley Judd can't handle the ins and outs of microbiology. Do we really care?

But wait, there's more. A-Rod's detractors have built up a pretty substantial chorus that solemnly offers the refrain that their $275 million guy can't hit in the clutch, one of those great baseball bromides that is traditionally used as the ultimate weapon to brandish when all else fails.

2005 Topps Cracker Jack

compelling presentation, but probably a popular sentiment among the players themselves, many of whom are lushly rewarded for a "talent" that may little more than an illusion and largely the product of selective perception.

"I could care less," Rodriguez insisted in a 2006 interview with Mark Feinsand. "I've done a lot of special things in this game, and for none of it to be considered clutch, it's an injustice. I don't take anything personally; I enjoy it, it motivates me and I think it's comical," he continued. "I think for anyone who drives in over 130 runs numerous times in his career, it's impossible not to be clutch."

I have even heard fans and television commentators offer that most of A-Rod's home runs come with the bases empty, which, of course, is the case with most players regardless of their clutch reputations. Facing the most imposing statistics in the game, one would suppose a pitcher would be loathe to serve up homer-worthy offerings with men on base, a truism for the likes of Rodriguez and all of the great sluggers in the game. But like the broader clutch hitter charge, it's a debate he's not likely to win.

A-Rod's record-setting 10-year, $252 million contract expired after the 2007 season, and after the typical kabuki dance between the Steinbrenners and A-Rod's agent, Scott Boras, all parties fairly quickly agreed to a "basic framework" for a brand-new 10-year jackpot. The new one was for $275 million, with the prospect of additional monies likely in store should he break the all-time home run record while in Yankee pinstripes.

Even through this process, Rodriguez took a beating from the New York press so gleefully inclined to administer same. And the timing of the newly announced deal, coming in the eighth inning of Game Four of the World Series as the Red Sox were unceremoniously dispatching the Colorado Rockies in a four-game sweep, was also criticized. This ill-advised timing was likened to that of perennial baseball black sheep Pete Rose, who upstaged the 2004 Hall of Fame election announcement with the release of his autobiography, "My Prison Without Bars," where he admitted – after denying it for 15 years – that he had bet on baseball.

Ultimately, it becomes one of those fun Hot Stove League talking points, since there's great disagreement in the baseball community about whether there's even such a thing as a clutch hitter. Fans insist that they've seen too many instances; baseball numbers guys, the SABRmaticians who have gained so much prominence in the years since free agency arrived, insist – not unanimously – that there is no such thing.

For this, A-Rod finds a defender in his teammate, Derek Jeter, who is widely regarded as a fine clutch hitter. "You can take those stat guys," Jeter told *Sports Illustrated*, "and throw them out the window." Not exactly a

That linkage seemed a tad unfair at the time, but probably small potatoes among the slings and arrows peppered at him by sportswriters. As the Yankees closed down their beloved Stadium in 2008 without so much as a Wild Card invitation into the postseason, the best player in the game was saddled with a label suggesting his presence on a team was antithetical to team chemistry.

In the face of a storybook season from a Tampa Bay Devil Rays club with the second-lowest payroll in MLB and a meltdown on Wall Street that elicited calls for taxpayer-financed bailouts in the hundreds of billions of dollars, bashing millionaires got new life and a newfound currency.

For the moment, at least, A-Rod will have to content himself with simply banking those millions while he awaits potential redemption in a World Series to be named later.

Collectors Corner: A-Rod's status in the world of the baseball card collector is a microcosm of his overall career. The ridiculous amount of money that so distorts the picture of Alex Rodriguez has no less of an impact for collectors.

A-Rod arrived on the MLB scene just as the baseball card industry was remaking itself – and its product – into something almost unrecognizable from that which had charmed earlier generations. Given the odd way that cards are made today, with a contrived scarcity goofily countered by the creation of preposterous numbers of different cards, and you have a curious and unsatisfying situation for collectors.

There are literally thousands of new cards of A-Rod, but many are terribly expensive because of the contrived scarcity mentioned above, and in any event trying to form a collection of all of them is almost literally impossible. And collectors can get pretty obsessive about getting their hands on everything available. His autograph, coveted by millions of fans, becomes a bone of contention for old-timers who are used to crouching behind stadium pillars or patiently encamping in the parking lot for a chance at a freebee.

When an A-Rod-signed item can instantly translate into hundreds or thousands of dollars in an eBay auction, its problematic for players to be doing much signing gratis. Initially regarded as a friendly signer when he first came up, his meteoric rise as a superstar would be in inverse relation to his availability in such informal settings.

"I don't mind this at all," Rodriguez said in a 2000 interview after signing yet another autograph for an adoring young fan. "I love kids and it's even fun for me. Their interest is unconditional. They day they stop asking for your autograph is the day you're in trouble."

That scary day obviously hasn't arrived – and probably never will – but changing economics have limited how often he might appear in a paid public setting. Indeed, Rodriguez conceded to another hobby writer that what had once been a good way "to pay the rent," was now something less than that, since he no longer needed the money.

It's hardly Rodriguez's fault, but a hobby that was so starkly transformed in the 1980s by the notion of paid autograph appearances for former players is likely to get transformed once again in coming years as the highly-paid stars of this generation retire. If this group of players winds up needing our autographing tithes in 10 years or so, we are all going to be in a lot of trouble.

2005 Heritage card.

2005 Topps Turkey
Red and 2008
Heritage cards.

Chapter 13

Barry Halper

I t only seems fitting that the greatest franchise in the history of Major League Baseball would be able to lay claim to the man deemed to be the greatest collector as well. It may have been the perfect marriage, aided somewhat by the fact that the collector in question was also a part-owner of the franchise itself.

Barry Halper, owner until the fall of 1999 of the most incredible collection of baseball memorabilia ever assembled, parlayed his minority ownership morsel of the New York Yankees into an unprecedented link between memorabilia collector and the very same players being collected.

For decades, they would take part in the holy pilgrimage to Halper's home in Livingston, N.J. There, after a suitable period of alternately gawking and gasping, they would sign this artifact or that. It was never quid pro quo; rather, it was simply a part of the liturgy of this singularly secular religion.

The home was modest and Barry Halper was modest, but that particular adjective probably never was directed at his lifelong accumulation of perhaps $40 million in baseball treasures. It was

This was the informal sign-in sheet when ballplayers would step into Barry's basement; below, a small sampling of pins and buttons.

assembled by Halper at a time perfectly suited to the undertaking, and it was done with a zeal and a reverence for the history of the game that will never be duplicated.

Halper, who died in December of 2005, almost single-handedly created the hobby of collecting sports memorabilia. Like most serious hobbyists, he started with cards, but he quickly whizzed past that phase: his interests resided with all of the artifacts that touched the players – and that they touched – and further, he wanted to get their signatures right along with them.

It started innocently enough with an 8-year-old youngster hanging around the clubhouse of the Newark Bears in 1947. Former Cub and Phillie Lou "The Mad Russian" Novikoff watched in amazement as the youth hustled about for autographs on every scorecard or program he could find. "Does your mother know that you're coming here?" the ballplayer asked. Assured that she did not, Novikoff promised something special the following day, perhaps in hopes that it might somehow satiate the boy's collecting appetite. Uh, huh.

The next day Novikoff tossed Halper a brown paper bag. Inside it was Barney McCosky's uniform. Just as when Joe Hardy made his Faustian pact in "Damn Yankees," this simple act sealed Halper's fate, though of course no damnation of any sort was involved.

The next year, Halper was at Yankee Stadium as the Yankees retired Babe's No. 3. "The Babe got out of his car, and I went under the barricade and asked him to sign this book on a blank page. He didn't talk, he just signed it," Halper recalled in a 1996 interview at his home.

A decade later when Halper went off to college at the University of Miami, he made the baseball team and astutely got team coach Jimmie Foxx to sign the same piece of paper. Foxx, in turn, suggested that Halper visit Mel Ott, who was slated to visit a while later. And just like that, Halper had embarked on his odyssey to collect signatures from the 500 Home Run Club, the prototype of dozens of similar unofficial groupings that owe as much to Barry Halper for their existence and popularity as they do to the erstwhile statistician.

The Barry Halper Collection would be patiently assembled over

It wasn't all Yankees, but they dominated here, just as at the Stadium.

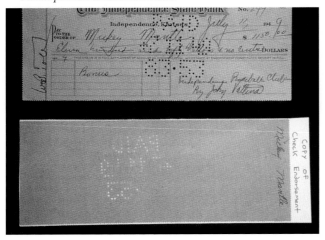

Lots of Gold and Cash, as in Gloves (above) and a Mickey Mantle personal check shown below.

the coming decades, with an exclusivity to baseball, the game he loved, and an informal emphasis on his beloved Yankees, many of whom he would befriend over the years.

The Yankee Clipper probably topped that list, which ran to literally hundreds of current and former ballplayers, and a good chunk of that number were New York Yankees.

After becoming a close confidant of The Yankee Clipper and welcoming him to his home and his basement shrine for many years, their friendship was upended in 1994 over what DiMaggio perceived as a slight concerning arrangements surrounding a DiMaggio-hosted tour of the Halper Collection.

"I called him on his birthday, opening day and at old-timer's games, but he doesn't acknowledge me," Halper continued with obvious sadness tinged in his voice. A mortified Halper would be snubbed by the Hall of Famer for several years before they reconciled without fanfare a couple of years before DiMaggio died.

Mickey Mantle also was a periodic visitor, and also understood the signing protocol ... sort of. "Mickey would sign anything," Halper said with a laugh, "but sometimes he would write things that can't be included in a family magazine." Or a book.

The author can vouch for that, having seen some of the pieces at Halper's home in Livingston in 1996, and later at Halper's new home in New Vernon, N.J., in 2004. The new digs, several light years more imposing than the home that housed his massive collection until 1999, was built largely on the proceeds from the 1999-2000 liquidation, which may have pushed up toward $40 million when all was said and done.

The Halper Collection Auction at Sotheby's topped $22 million that September of 1999, and several million dollars more was sold over the Internet over the next year. Halper had also sold more than $5 million of his primo stuff (really, it all was) to Major League Baseball prior to the Halper Auction at Sotheby's. MLB quietly turned the material over to the Baseball Hall of Fame, which was thrilled to have such treasures added to their sacred stash.

For obvious reasons, the Hall of Fame has always resisted the

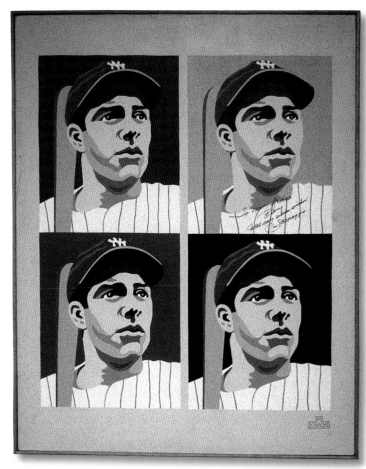

The elegant original artwork of Joe DiMaggio by acclaimed artist Michael Schacht found the perfect home in Halper's Collection.

impulse to set a precedent of buying memorabilia, rather than insisting on donations from the players and their families. It was a sound strategy in the last millennium, and it's even sounder these days.

Competing in the frenzied marketplace so prominently sculpted by Barry Halper is no place for a nonprofit organization that likes to earmark its ample annual endowments toward educational efforts rather than arm wrestling with well-heeled memorabilia collectors.

In the later years, Halper himself was confronted with something of a similar nature. Occasionally criticized for getting material donated by players and/or their families and yet later selling those items at often eye-popping profits, Halper conceded that while he did get some things for a song, it was hardly the norm, especially at the end.

"I hear criticism that that's not right, since I had things given to me," Halper noted in an interview prior to the 1999 auction. "That was my ingenuity if I got something for nothing, but believe me, I paid for a lot of things, too."

What all that ingenuity – and cash, much of it from his family-owned printing business in New Jersey – yielded was this sampling from the famed 1999 auction: 400 bats, including Joe Jackson's Black Betsy; 1,800 signed baseballs, 30,000 cards (as noted earlier, they were almost an afterthought by then); 1,000 uniforms that were housed in an enclosed, electronic compartment that would be the envy of any dry-cleaning establishment); 4,000 photos; 1,000 player contracts, 4,500 personal papers, and thousands of other pieces, like

And so it begins, the historic sale of the Halper Collection at Sotheby's in September of 1999.

press pins, plaques and trophies, and even Ty Cobb's dentures.

One of the players from outside his beloved Yankees realm who visited Halper's basement in the early 1980s was Pete Rose, who had donated several items to the Hall of Fame and in return received a silver "Lifetime Donor Pass" that provided admittance to the Hall at any time.

In customary Rose fashion, he flipped the card to his friend, Barry Halper, and even conceded to sign and inscribe it, per Halper house tradition. "I shouldn't need this thing to get into the Hall of Fame," it said, followed by Pete's signature. Hmmm.

Barry's already there in spades. Pete might have wanted to hang on to that one item.

Mickey signed this one for sure.

Sotheby's/Barry Halper

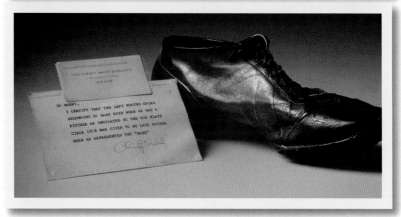

A corner of Barry's basement (top), his vast vault of jerseys (center) and Babe Ruth's bronzed pitching spikes.

Last photo Sotheby's/Barry Halper

No baseball fan on Earth ever revered Babe Ruth more than Barry Halper did, and he had the collection to prove it.

Sotheby's/Barry Halper

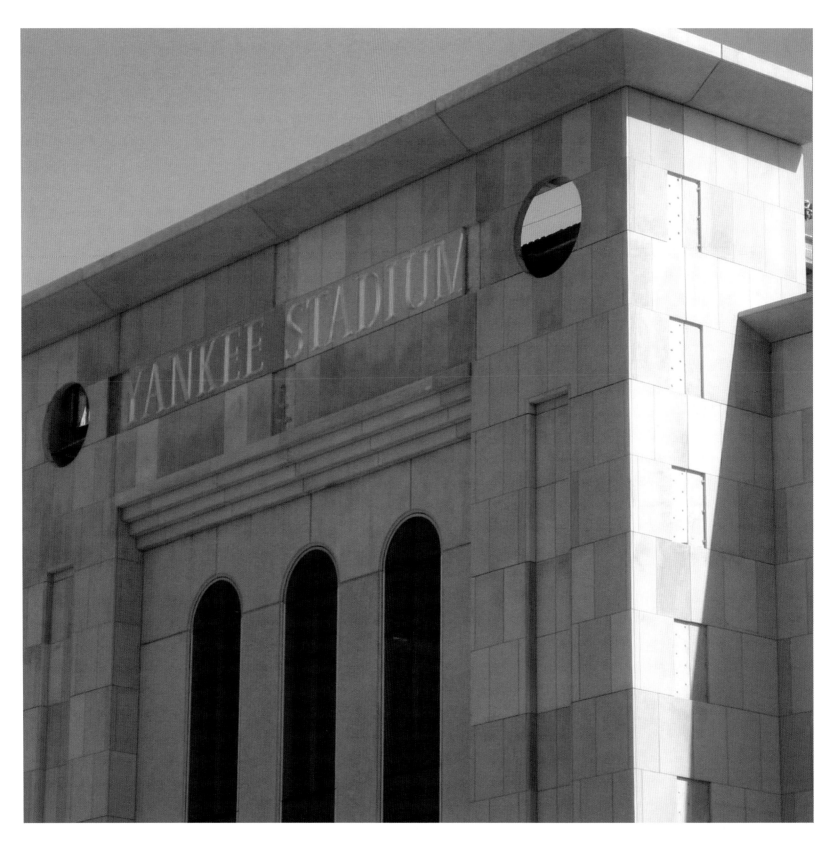

Chapter 14

The New Yankee Stadium

By the time the end of the Yankees' 30-year lease was approaching in the mid-1990s, the team had returned to a position of some prominence in the American League, though hardly reflective of the dominance that was to come.

Amid the glow of an improbable World Series triumph in 1996 that marked the club's first in nearly two decades, George Steinbrenner started to do his best Walter O'Malley impression by grumbling about attendance while he looked longingly at glitzy new ballparks being built in Baltimore and Cleveland.

The numbers at the aging Stadium were hardly chopped liver: in 15 of the previous 20 years the club had drawn more than 2 million fans. Numbers like that put the team roughly in the middle of the pack in the intensifying scrum for American League fans, a position Steinbrenner insisted was thoroughly inadequate at a time when the egalitarian notion of revenue sharing was slated to begin in 1997.

So the drumbeat for a new ballpark, given life perhaps initially by threats – veiled or otherwise – in the 1980s that the club would relocate to New Jersey, grew into an almost funereal dirge by the time

Yankees final dynasty of the 20th century was in full flower.

The "options" ostensibly included relocating to the West Side Railyard site, an idea from the 1980s originally championed by then New York State Governor Mario Cuomo. With the Metropolitan Transportation Authority quickly chiming in that merely providing the concrete platform upon which to build a new stadium would cost $200 million (estimated at the time), and the all-purpose domed stadium might run to $1.1 billion, the dream was pretty quickly dismissed.

Which left moving to the 97-acre site occupied by Yonkers Raceway (Yonkers Yankees kind of rolls off the tongue, doesn't it?) or, more likely, following the football Giants and Jets to the alluring siren call of the Meadowlands in New Jersey.

Yonkers is Yonkers, and there is also the problem of access roads from both Westchester and Connecticut, and New Jersey fans would

Construction is underway on the "New" Stadium.

still be saddled with the need to traverse the George Washington Bridge and the dreaded Major Deegan Expressway. And though the author is a former Yonkeranian (I made the word up; P.S. 25 fifth-grader in 1960), it's hard to imagine displacing the harness racing empire was ever much more than a bargaining chip.

The Meadowlands was almost certainly the biggest threat that the Yankees had, but it never really materialized either. Ultimately, most fans realized that while the Giants or Jets could be effectively transplanted westward, the Yankees' history and mystique precluded such a move.

Besides, back at Gracie Mansion Steinbrenner had the ally he needed: Mayor Rudy Giuliani. Shortly before leaving office in December of 2001, America's Mayor announced tentative agreements for both the Mets and Yankees that would have had the city picking up half of the costs for construction, estimated at nearly $800 million, along with half again that number for transportation improvements

Building major league stadiums in any city in the country is a gargantuan undertaking that almost universally costs more than originally envisioned, but the current plans call for the new Yankee Stadium to be a $1.3 billion project on the 22 acres of Macombs Dam Park and John Mullaly Park, the latter of which was already used by the former Stadium for parking on game days. Many experts insisted that the final tally is more likely to approach $1.6 billion.

The city retains ownership of the land, and will not charge the Yankees rent or property taxes. Reports pin the cost of renovating the existing parkland at around $25 million, with another $150 million earmarked for new parkland.

The demolition costs are included in that figure, and are to be borne by the City and replaced with parkland.

And while the details of the demolition of the old park are still being debated by New York City officials, there has already been a bit of mischief in the new one that required some pesky alterations in some already-finished sections.

A construction worker who apparently is also an avid fan of

the hated rivals the Red Sox, buried a replica David Ortiz jersey in the concrete underneath the visitors dugout, the treachery clearly designed at placing a curse on the new ballpark. It's not clear why Bosox fans would still be fuming about some old Curse of the Bambino, since that noxious bit of supernatural nuttiness was presumably laid to rest in 2004.

Exposed by co-workers, the Yankees went to the considerable expense of digging this ersatz artifact up, and promptly donated it to the Jimmy Fund, the Red Sox' favored charity started in 1948 by the other Boston team, the National League Braves, which left town five years later.

The Jimmy Fund sold the Ortiz jersey in a charity auction, netting $175,000 and presumably recording the all-time record price for an unofficial, non-game-used jersey. The construction worker who caused all this mayhem – and subsequent windfall for the fight against cancer in children – has insisted he has planted other items, like a 2004 ALCS scorecard and program, but isn't fessing up to any locations.

Isn't a $1.6 billion price tag (and rising?) enough of a curse for any new stadium?

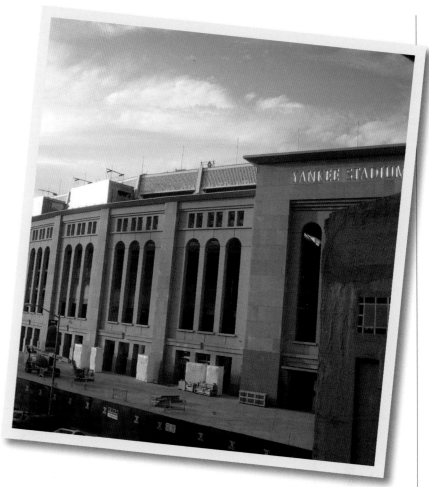

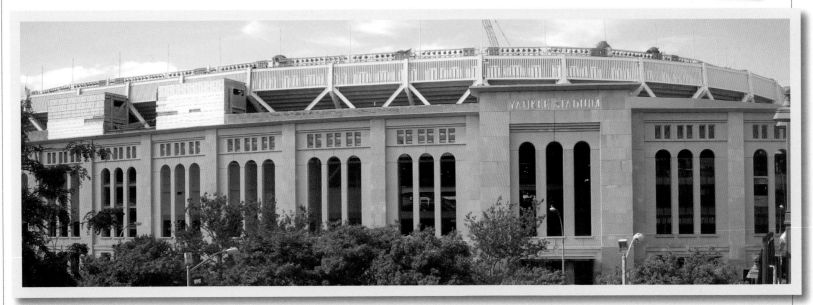

Acknowledgments

Calling this "my book" is no less absurd than suggesting that a successful major-league baseball campaign might be the product of a savvy manager or star player. I rounded up all this stuff and put it in my own words, but the vast battalion of editors, writers, artists, photographers, hobby officials and news organizations all contributed mightily in various ways.

F + W Media book editors Paul Kennedy and Joe Kertzman get the first nod for coming up with the idea in the first place, and Justin Moen warrants the next as the principal editor of the book itself. Heidi Bittner-Zastrow designed it in a fashion that speaks for itself in terms of the elegance and importance of her contribution.

Further down I list reference sources from authors and writers, artists and photographers, auction houses and hobby manufacturers; also included is a listing of books and websites utilized in the research of this book. Each section is listed in alphabetical order, since attempting to quantify or qualitatively rank contributions is essentially impossible.

I first take note of a number of friends, interview subjects, and professional colleagues who contributed to the success of this huge undertaking but defy easy categorization: Doug Allen, Marty Appel, Sy Berger, Yogi Berra, Levi Bleam, Dave Bushing, Larry Canale, Gary Cypres, Dave Czuba, Josh Evans, Bob Feller, Whitey Ford, Jeff and Larry Fritsch, Michael Gershman, Michael Gidwitz, Bill Goodwin, Dick Gordon, Cheryl Goyda, Barry Halper, Brad Horn, Michael Heffner, David Hunt, Reggie Jackson, Andy Jurinko, Jeff Idelson, Roger Kahn, Kevin Keating, Irv Lerner, Rob Lifson, Clay Luraschi, Bill Mastro, Ernie Montella, Keith Olbermann, Bert Padell, Dick Perez, Alan Rosen, Kevin Savage, Christina Schenk, Pete Siegel, Jimmy Spence, Frank and Peggy Steele, Randall Swearingen, Frank Torre, Joe Walsh, Stephen Wong, and Kit Young.

Photo Credits and References

Artists and photographers: Charles De Simone, William Feldman, James Fiorentino, Bill Gallo, Jerry Hersh, Ronnie Joyner, Paul Madden, Arthur K. Miller, Bill Purdom, Phil Sarno, Mike Schacht, Monty Sheldon, Robert Stephen Simon, David Spindel, Bruce Stark, Ron Stark, Darryl Vlasak, Bill Williams, Steve Wolf, and Leslie Woods

Companies and auction houses that provided photo access: Donruss, Fleer, Gartlan Collectibles, Bill Goff, Guernsey's Auctions, Grey Flannel Auctions, Hartland Collectibles, Heritage Auction Galleries, Huggins & Scott Auctions, Hunt Auctions, Lelands.com, Mastro Auctions, Memory Lane Inc., Robert Edward Auctions, SCP Auctions, Sotheby's, Steiner Sports Marketing, The Topps Co., and The Upper Deck Co.

Sports Collectors Digest **contributors and F+W Media editors:** Greg Ambrosius, Tom Bartsch, Steve Bloedow, Mike Breeden, David Craft, Lou Criscione, Brian Earnest, William Felchner, Paul Ferrante, Rick Firfer, Ross Forman, Scott Fragale, Robert Grayson, Kevin Huard, Tom Hultman, Scott Kelnhofer, Ted Kietlinski, Doug Koztoski, Rocky Landsverk, Ed Lucas, Rich Marazzi, Tom Mortenson, Kevin Nelson, Chris Nerat, Robert Obojski, Paul Post, Justin Priddy, Dan Schlossberg and David Seideman

Reference sources: Associated Press, www.baseball-almanac.com, The Baseball Encyclopedia, www.baseballhalloffame.org, www.baseballlibrary.com, www.baseballreference.com, www.ESPN.com, www.mickeyrivers.com, www.nytimes.com, www.operationbullpen.com, www.sportscollectorsdigest.com, www.sportscolumn.com, USA Today Yankee Stadium, and Wikipedia, the free encyclopedia.

And finally, a word of appreciation to my bosses at *Sports Collectors Digest*, group publisher Jeff Pozorski and sports division publisher Dean Listle, both of whom agreed to allow me to write this book. Though relegated to evenings and weekends, some of the time extracted for this massive project inevitably came from time that would have been directed at the magazine. Their forbearance is appreciated.

– T.S. O'Connell

Expand Your Passion for the Game

2009 Standard Catalog of® Baseball Cards
18th Edition
by Don Fluckinger

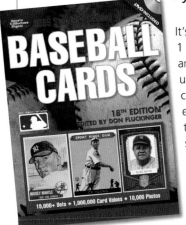

It's big in size and complete in coverage, with 1 million listings for vintage and modern cards and real-world collector pricing this book is undoubtedly the ultimate guide to baseball cards. Updated each fall, this guide's coverage extends from cards issued in the mid-1800s to 2008 and includes 15,000 sets representing Tobacco and Bubblegum cards and Specialty issue. A bonus DVD features PDFs of the pages, with key word search and page enlargement capabilities.

Item# Z2044 • $44.99

The Essential SCD:
A Sports Collectors Guide to Authentication, Grading & Fraud CD
From the Editors of *Sports Collectors Digest*

Search 30 informative and inspiring stories written by the best journalists and researchers of the sports collecting hobby, on this one-of-a-kind CD and find reliable facts and advice about spotting fakes, grading with expertise and authenticating with confidence. Get news you can use about leading autograph subjects, including Ruth, Cobb, Gehrig and others, along with authenticating tips from leading experts.

CD-ROM • Item# Z4265 • $12.99

500 Great Baseball Cards CD
by Rocky Landsverk

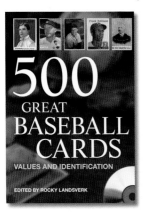

Whether you collect by team, era, brand, or any other card combination, there's always a select group that top the list of the most desirable. That's what you'll find in this fantastic CD of the 500 greatest of the game, and the couture of card collecting. Each card is featured in a full-color or black and white photo that's easily enlargeable to see detail, along with current collector pricing – straight from the experts at *Sports Collectors Digest* and *Tuff Stuff's Sports Collectors Monthly*.

CD-ROM • Item# Z4966 • $12.99

The Everything Kids' Baseball Book, 5th Ed.
By Greg Jacobs

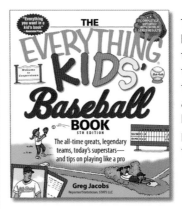

This book covers all the bases of the big league game, baseball history and trivia of the players, places and points that make the game great. Identify your favorite players, rookies and big-league all-stars, study the statistics and record-breaking plays, take in the history of ballparks around the country and learn how to set up a fantasy baseball team.

Item# Z1418 • $7.95